COLD COMFORT

Essays by

CHRISTY LORIO

BELLE POINT PRESS

Fort Smith, Arkansas

Cold Comfort

Edited by Casie Dodd
Design & typography by Belle Point Press

Belle Point Press
Fort Smith, Arkansas
bellepointpress.com
editor@bellepointpress.com

Printed in the United States of America

26 25 24 23 22 3 4 5 6 7

ISBN: 979-8-9858965-7-2

CC/BPP4

Contents

To Ricky

June 2001	Dad dies from colorectal cancer one year after his diagnosis.
June 2018	I'm diagnosed with stage-IV colorectal cancer after having a seizure from a brain metastasis.
July 2018	Craniotomy, gamma knife (radiation surgery).
August 2018	Start first round of chemo.
March 2019	Pelvic radiation, niece is born on Mardi Gras Day—a week later: lower anterior resection surgery with a temporary ileostomy bag.
May 2019	Ileostomy bag removal.
October 2019	Rediagnosed: cancer spreads to lung, start chemo again.
May 2020	Graduate from first grad program (MFA Creative Writing).
July 2020	Lung radiation.
August 2020	Begin second grad program (MFA Studio Art).
November 2020	Find out cancer didn't go away, now on chemo for life; also diagnosed with stage-0 melanoma.
January 2022	Brain tumor recurrence, gamma knife for the third time.
May 2022	Vision starts to go haywire, diagnosed with Parinaud Syndrome.
August 2022	Diagnosed with Leptomeningeal Disease (LMD)—prognosis: six months to live.

* The first printing of *Cold Comfort* was published November 15, 2022. On November 29, Christy passed away peacefully at home surrounded by loved ones.

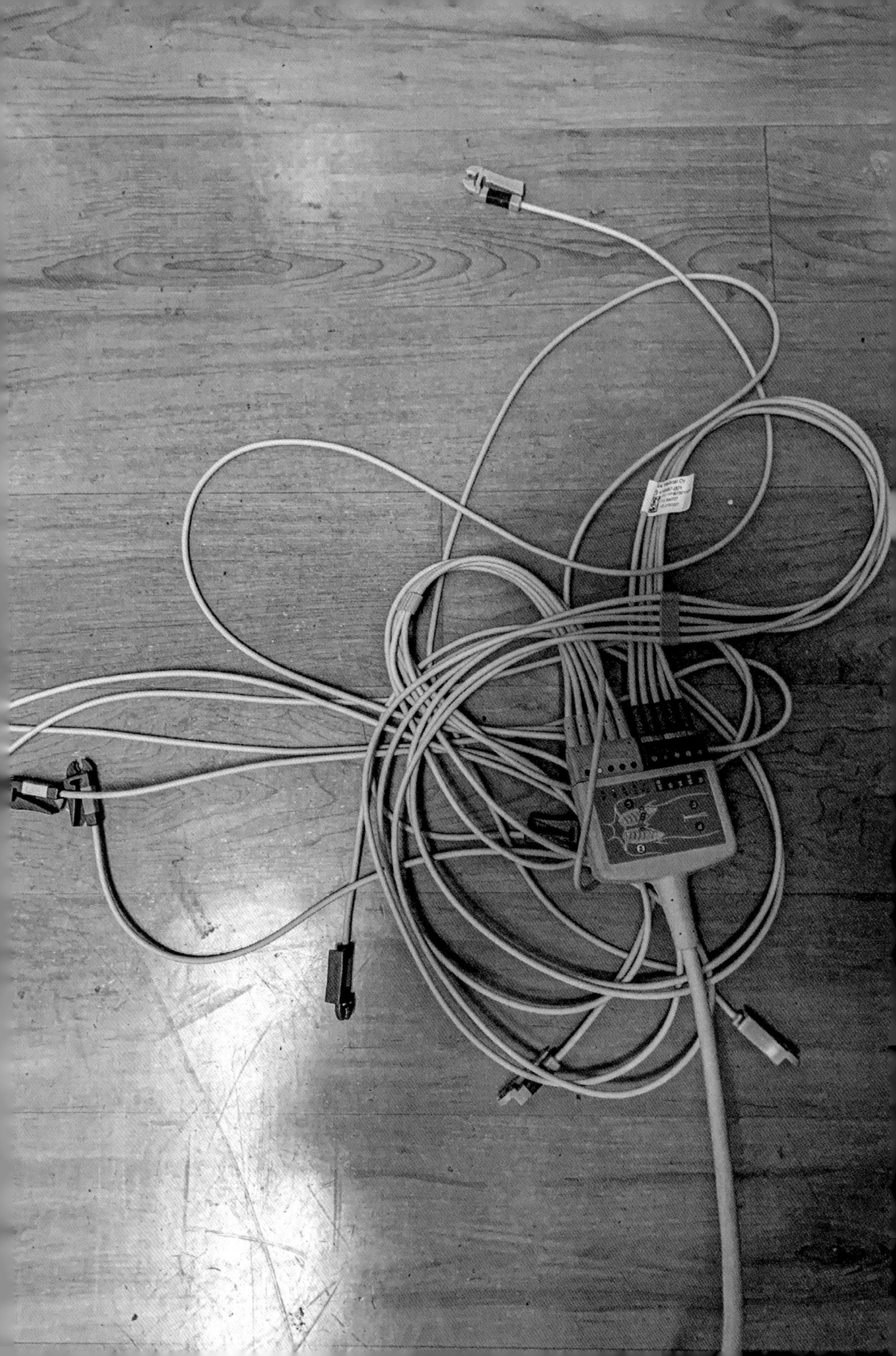

Port Access

I never get used to feeling a needle plunge into my chest, even though I've been subjected to it almost every other week for four years. A port, or port-o-cath, is a device inserted beneath the skin to administer drugs. The only external indicator that I have one is a sliver of a horizontal scar between my collar bone and right breast.

The first surgery I ever had was brain surgery. I wasn't bothered by the procedure. It was more of a relief that I was going to start addressing the cancer, after having been trapped in a hospital in Cork, Ireland, for a week after my unexpected seizure. Prior to that day, I thought I was perfectly healthy. I was subjected to a litany of medical tests. I shared with the hospital staff that my dad died from colorectal cancer, which prompted them to order a colonoscopy. The doctors were "99 percent sure" they wouldn't find anything. When I woke up from anesthesia, I found out I had stage-IV rectal cancer. I stayed in the hospital for a few more days; then I had to wait a week for a flight back home, which was a prolonged waiting period until treatment. When I arrived back in the States two weeks later, my medical team rushed to get me care. I flew back to New Orleans, and the next day I saw an oncologist, a colorectal surgeon, and a neurosurgeon. On July 5, 2018, I had my craniotomy.

You'd think I'd have been petrified of having my skull cracked open, but I was relieved to get this damn tumor out of my head. The recovery was hard, but getting my port placed was a true mind fuck. I remember my dad had a port, which is why getting my own was immensely difficult. My dad died a year after his diagnosis. At first, my brain tumor felt like an anomaly. The port solidified that I was about to be blasted with chemotherapy.

The port-o-cath surgery was a mild one. I went home the same day and was only sedated enough to calm me down, not put me under. Still, I cried the entire time as the surgeon placed my port, which looks vaguely similar to a Ouija board planchette with a catheter that is threaded into the superior vena cava, a large vein on the right side of the heart. My chest was still black and blue from the surgery when I went back to the cancer center for my first round of chemo. I wailed in the waiting room. I was so scared, unsure what the toxins would do to me. Another cancer patient came to console me, which was sweet. *That's it: I'm officially in this club*. At thirty-eight years old, this wasn't what I expected my life to be like.

In the infusion center, a nurse explained the entire process to me. My husband, Thomas, and my mom were there, offering support. I felt bad that my mom had to go through this again with someone else she loved. The nurse opened up her kit, which contained a cleaning pad, a saline flush, and the needle and dressing. "Lean back into the chair and relax," the nurse said. The needle sliced through my bruised chest, which left me howling in pain. The needle made contact with the port, which would guide the toxins through an I.V. bag, which would then dispense the chemo throughout my body with each pump of my heart.

A social worker came to discuss financial options with me. My health insurance situation was complicated: I was in grad school and on my school's student health-care plan, so dropping out of school wasn't an option. But I wouldn't be able to drive for six months after my seizure, so we worked on finding grants to pay for daily ride shares to campus. I also worked as a graduate assistant, which paid for my tuition so long as I was enrolled full-time. All of this meant that I would have to remain a full-time student and part-time graduate assistant while enduring the hardest thing I've ever had to do. But all that was weeks away, and I needed to live day by day in order to get through cancer treatment.

I dozed off as the drugs entered my system for the first time. Aside from the needle stick, the infusion was without incident.

I was sent home with a chemo pump—a rectangular contraption that would disperse a second chemo drug over the next forty-six hours. The chemo pump made a soft whirring sound, which I could drown out with music during the day. Come bedtime, sleep proved difficult as the machine's noises kept me awake. A tangle of I.V. cords tethered me to the pump while that damn needle was embedded in my chest.

I was off and on the chemo pump for two years before I decided to switch to Xeloda, the same drug but in pill form. Xeloda has worse side effects, which is why I was so reticent to make the change. Diarrhea and more fatigue plagued me. Hand and foot syndrome was miserable. Still, the agony of schlepping the pump around, mixed with the sleepless nights, made my decision worth it.

Until recently, my port was accessed every other week for my Avastin infusions, a drug that helps chemo work better. I learned to cope with getting my port accessed. Lidocaine spray helps numb the area, so I started to douse myself with it an hour before my infusion appointment. It helped, but the needle still hurt. I tried to talk to the nurses while they stabbed me to distract myself. I always turned my head and looked away, trying to fixate on the television, a ceiling tile—anything that took me out of the moment. It was a brutal reminder that I'm sick, but a necessary one.

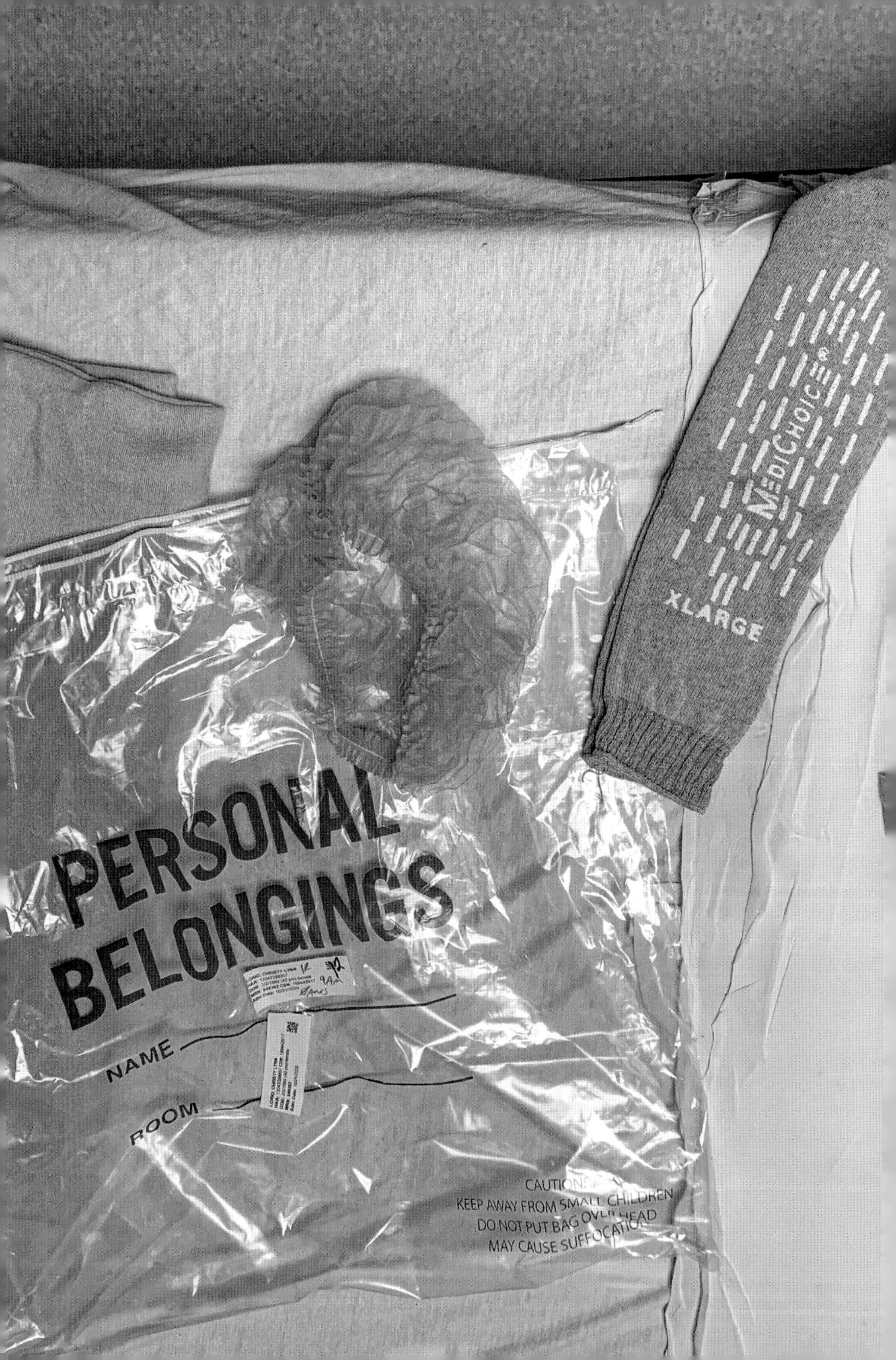
MEDICHOICE
XLARGE
PERSONAL
BELONGINGS
NAME
ROOM
CAUTION
KEEP AWAY FROM SMALL CHILDREN
DO NOT PUT BAG OVER HEAD
MAY CAUSE SUFFOCATION

Clothes

CLOTHING has always been an important way for me to outwardly express myself. My mom likes to tell a story of when I was a toddler. I was shopping with her, saw a pretty dress, grabbed it and proclaimed "Mine!" Nothing much has changed, except I have more impulse control. In eighth grade, I lusted over Doc Marten boots. My mom wouldn't spring for a pair, so I got Payless knock offs instead. Still, I loved those boots. Middle school and high school were formative times for me. I didn't want to fit in with the preppy girls (and I couldn't), so I veered into the '90s grunge trend. I favored thrift store finds and whatever I could score on clearance at stores like Gadzooks and Hot Topic.

When I was hospitalized for a week in Ireland, all I had on me when I was admitted were the clothes on my back, two cell phones (one from home and one for Ireland), and a small notebook and pen. I wasn't planning on being there, obviously. After a day or two, my boss grabbed clothes for me to wear out of our shared campus apartment; asking your boss to go through your underwear makes for a humiliating experience. Instead of a hospital gown, my days were spent in leggings and tank tops—something I usually only wear to the gym—but I was grateful to wear my own clothes. Doing so reminded me that I was still human—that I was still me. Hospital gowns have a way of reducing you down to being just a patient.

I met a friend for lunch shortly after I got back to New Orleans. I wore my cheeriest sundress, with punchy colored stripes. It was my way of lightening the mood. I don't feel good about myself if I'm wearing something dumpy or unflattering. I hate being uncomfortable, but I always want to look my best.

I rarely, if ever, go out in public in sweatpants. Even if I'm inside my own house all day, I don't feel productive if I'm sitting in my pajamas. I don't feel right. Only when I feel like complete shit do I stay in my pajamas all day, like a few days ago. My feet were so inflamed from chemo that it hurt to stand up, much less walk. I watched trashy reality TV and cult documentaries all day. I was in so much pain, the last thing I wanted to do was walk upstairs to change into real clothes.

I hear "you look great" a lot. Most people think cancer patients look frail and sickly, but that's just not the case. Most of the cancer patients I know look like everyone else. We're young and vibrant, which contributes to people thinking we are better off than we actually are. Most people have no idea how much I suffer. It waxes and wanes. Some days I feel great, and other days I can hardly get off the couch.

I have a friend—a fellow writer and cancer patient—who ascribes to a similar mindset. I visited her in the hospital a few weeks ago. I was at the cancer center for my regular oncologist appointment; she was in the hospital for a tumor in her spine that was causing her intense pain. She wore a punchy, flowy dress, and her walker was covered in fake flowers and streamers a la a kid's birthday party. As I talked to her, I asked myself: *How does she do it—how does she remain cheerful despite all of her suffering*? I often wonder these things about people in similar situations to mine. I never know what to tell people when they express that I'm an "inspiration" to them. Then I see people like Suzanne, and I remember that I'm no different from her.

I don't buy clothes out of season anymore. It's morbid, but I can't help but think: *What if I'm not around in six to eight months?* I don't like wasting money on clothing I don't wear. Buying clothing that I can't wear until the following season seems frivolous. That said, I'm all about treating myself when I need a morale boost. I don't splurge on designer clothes, but I do like to buy a few new clothing items every season to inject something fresh and fun into my wardrobe. When your life exists in the dark spots, you need to interject brightness into your life as much as possible.

Sometimes I think about what will become of my clothes when I'm gone. Will Thomas get rid of them quickly, or will he hang on to them—like precious reminders of a life lived? I have a few of my dad's old favorite T-shirts. There's one with bears and another with eagles, shirts he picked up as souvenirs on vacation. My two favorite shirts of his are one with an alligator that says "Louisiana Yard Dog" and a burgundy shirt that says "Cajun" in bold yellow lettering with a gator stirring a gumbo pot. The shirts are far too big for me, but I don't care. I wear them with pride. I find comfort in having these T-shirts. They're a reminder of my dad—who died when I was twenty-one—but more importantly, they're reminders of his personality and interests. I hope that when I'm gone, whoever inherits my stuff can feel good about those items, not sad. I've joked about being buried in a Mardi Gras costume and my roller skates. If I'm not cremated, I probably will request to be buried in a costume, but I want someone else to enjoy my skates. They bring me so much joy; I'd like to think they are infused with good energy, something that will heal and comfort whoever needs them.

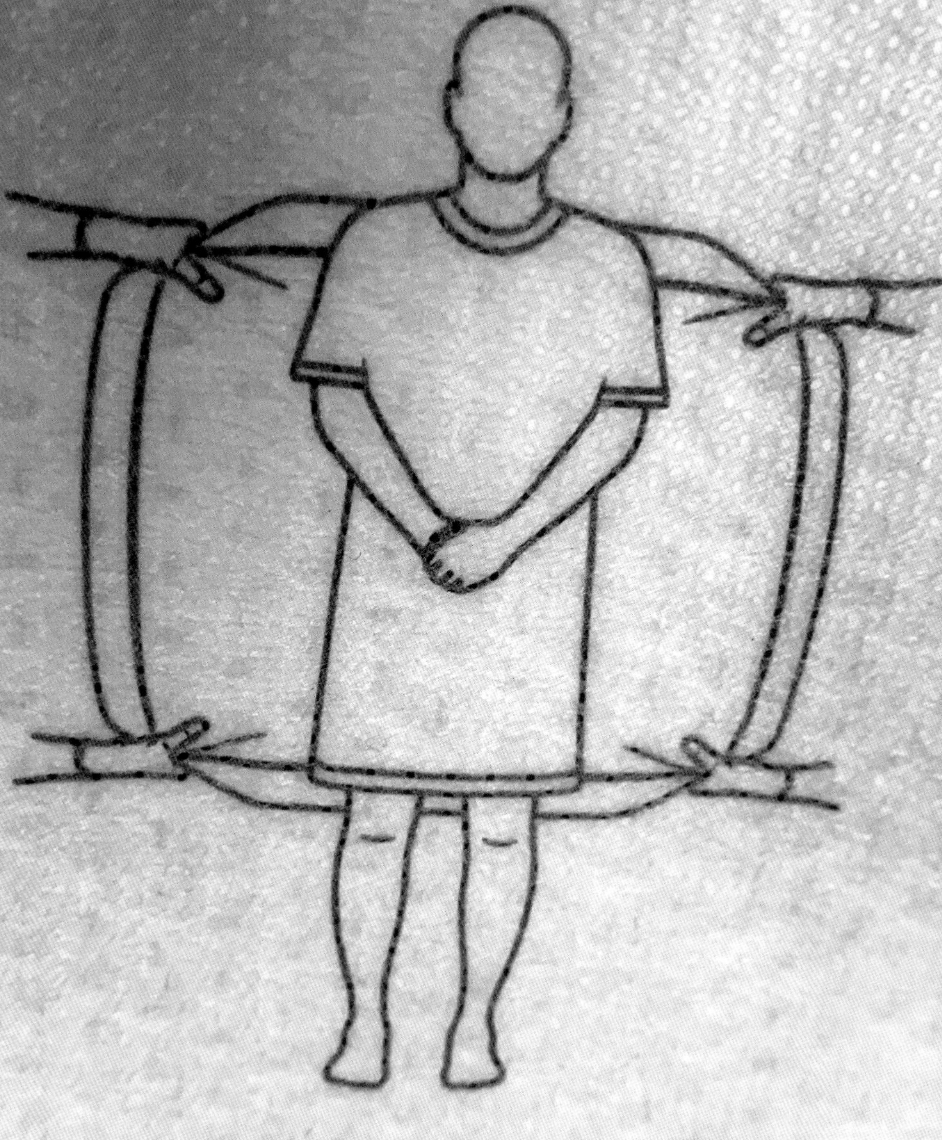

Death

I'm not afraid of death. I'm afraid of suffering. Death doesn't hurt. We're gone, and our surviving loved ones are left with the grief—the bone-deep pain. The transition is the scary part.

Thomas and I make jokes about me dying all the time. It's a release of the pressure valve. I've always had a dark sense of humor—a sort of coping mechanism. I've always been that person who laughs at inappropriate times when dealing with something intense. When I was a manager at a clothing store, I'd inevitably laugh when the shit hit the fan. Oh, how I wish I had innocuous things to laugh about again.

I've known a few cancer patients that have died. They were around my age, diagnosed roughly around the same time I was. It's unsettling, but I also think, *Well, statistically I'm sticking around*. That easily could have been me. I'd like to get to the ten-year mark—I'm currently at four. I know it's a stretch, but I do hear about people with stage-IV cancer living ten, even twenty years. It's rare, but it happens. Unfortunately, last week my doctors told me I have less than six months to live, so it looks like that won't be happening for me.

I learned of my friend Laura's death while I was at a writing residency. She was a few years younger than me. We met online about fifteen years ago, when I was heavy into fashion blogging and she was heavy into making jewelry. I interviewed her, and we kept up with each other on social media. I was diagnosed first, then she was diagnosed with the same cancer a year later. Her cancer was far more advanced than mine, even though we were both stage IV. She is from New Orleans but lived in Chattanooga, Tennessee, for a long time. She moved back to New Orleans to be closer to family, and I met her in person for the first time at her lovely, antiques-filled home. We shared the same oncologist, and I felt like I'd known her forever. We joked, we got serious; it was delightful to meet her in person after all those years, despite the circumstances. We would message each other, expressing our frustrations and small wins. I hadn't heard from her in a while, so I messaged her in the middle of the night this past January. Then I Googled her name. Her obituary immediately popped up: she had died on Christmas Day. Tears instantly streamed down my face. I was devastated. I cried for her, but I also cried for myself. Losing a friend to cancer when you also have cancer feels extra personal. I ran through the "what if that was me" scenario while also mourning my friend. I imagined what it would feel like to die. Was it any more miserable than anything else she went through? Was it scary? Or was she ready to go, desperate for her suffering to end?

My psychologist, who specializes in oncology patients, told me not to play out situations in my head that may or may not apply to me. It would only give me more anxiety. She's right, but I can't help myself in certain situations. I don't want to get blindsided; I don't want to pretend like everything will be okay when it most likely will not. I hope my tumors go away by some miracle, but I'm probably stuck with them until I die. My neurosurgeon told me that I will be plagued with brain tumor recurrences as long as I'm alive. I'd hoped that wouldn't be the case, that my brain tumors were an anomaly. It's already so hard to live with this, going through life like everything is okay when it is not.

Then things got even more not okay.

I was recently diagnosed with leptomeningeal disease. Only 5 percent of all cancer patients develop this. Lucky me. Leptomeningeal disease, or LMD, develops in late-stage cancer patients. I now have tumors in the lining of my brain. There is no cure and the treatment options are ineffective—hence my six-month prognosis. My radiologist said most people with LMD die in their sleep. That's cold comfort for a forty-two-year-old.

When people ask me how I'm doing, I tell them *As good as I can be* or *I'm okay*. I don't sugarcoat my reality, but I also don't want to have an entire conversation about my health with every person I come into contact with. It's unnecessary, and I don't want to dominate the conversation. Sometimes I just want to feel like a normal human being, even though I am very much not one.

Before my LMD diagnosis, I tried not to dwell in the dark place. I didn't obsess over death; I was too busy being fiercely alive. Still, I didn't make a lot of long-term goals for myself, but I did make shorter, attainable ones. There is so much I still want to do. I want to write a book. I want to keep building up my small photography business. I want to stick around long enough for my niece to get old enough to sleep at Aunt Christy's house. I dream about travel plans, hoping that I get to visit some of the places I've longed to see. I've learned only to book trips if I can get my money back in case something happens. Now I don't even do that.

Aside from LMD, I've been coasting for a while. My lung tumor and the affected lymph nodes have remained stable. I'd much rather have them go away, but stable is good news when you're terminally ill. The cancer hasn't spread to any other organs except my brain and lungs—yet. Now my brain is going to kill me.

People tell me all the time that I'm brave or inspirational to them. I don't see myself that way. I think people say that because they imagine themselves in my position. Maybe they're imagining that treatment isn't really that bad. I'm here to tell you that it is. I've had two people over the past year tell me, "Everyone dies," which is the most callous thing you can say to a cancer patient. Yes, we're all well aware that everyone dies. But it's another thing entirely to face your own mortality on a daily basis, especially when you're young. I try to pretend I'm elderly sometimes, to get in that mindset that any day now, it might be my time.

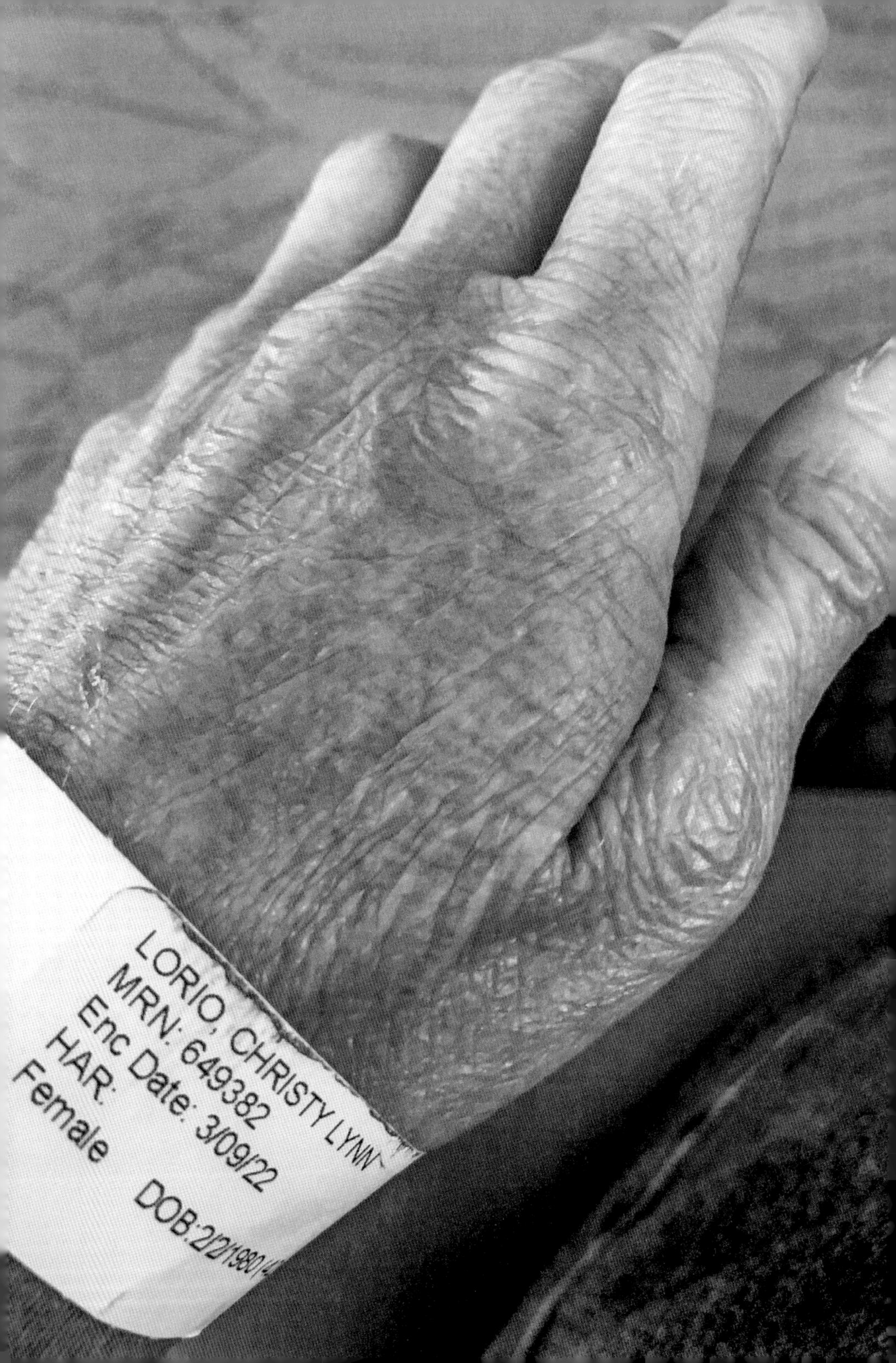
LORIO, CHRISTY LYNN
MRN: 649382
Enc Date: 3/09/22
HAR:
Female DOB:2/2/1980

Hand and Foot

Hand and foot syndrome is annoying at best and debilitating at worst. It's caused by chemo treatments. The skin on my hands and feet peel, which is unsightly but painless. My hands get bone dry; no amount of lotion seems to help. My feet have improved now that I use a thick cream twice a day and wear socks to keep in the moisture. I've stopped walking around my house barefoot; I've started wearing squishy slides, which helps immensely.

My hands resemble an eighty-year-old woman's. They are wrinkled and often inflamed—bright red like an apple. The inflammation makes the palms of my hands and the bottoms of my feet feel like rope burn, even on the gentlest of surfaces.

Last fall, Thomas and I went to Pensacola, Florida, for a quick getaway with our dog Beignet. We found an adventure zone, replete with go-karts, a zip line, and rock climbing. I was used to rock climbing on real rocks, not a plastic wall. My hands were so inflamed that day I could barely get off the ground. It's moments like these that are devastating.

The same thing goes for my feet. I wear the thickest socks and sneakers on the really bad days. It sounds vain, but I have to plan my outfits around my shoe choice when my feet are throbbing. We have a seagrass rug in our upstairs hallway, which is torture on my bare feet. I should just get rid of it, but I hate being wasteful. Instead, I tiptoe around it when my feet are flaring up. It's a ridiculous little dance I do when it would be so much easier to get rid of the damn rug.

I try not to let any part of my cancer experience rule my life, but it gets harder and harder not to as I progress further in treatment. I'm approaching a hundred rounds of chemo over four years. The chemo is keeping me alive, but it also breaks me down. I've shifted my mentality since I know I'm on this poison for the rest of my life. It's not that I've given up hope; I just don't want to lie to myself. I was in denial when my dad died—when his chemo and surgeries failed him. A surgeon told my mom that he would be back on the golf course a week after his liver operation. He was dead a week later. I don't want to blindside myself like that again. Twenty-one years ago, I was in deep denial of how sick my dad was; I couldn't admit it to myself. If I did, I thought I would damn him. Looking back, I could have handled my dad's death better. I was twenty-one at the time; I could have handled my entire life better, but I don't regret anything. It wasn't my fault. It wasn't anyone's fault.

I usually try to rest as much as I can when I'm experiencing a flare-up. I can sometimes anticipate when I'll have one, such as on a particularly active day. Still, there is no definite science to determine how my body will respond. Last summer, for example, we hiked the Grandview Trail in the Grand Canyon, which can be very challenging even for healthy hikers. I did it on a chemo week, yet somehow my feet didn't flare up even though I hiked a brutal six-mile round trip. That just shows you how unpredictable cancer treatment can be.

I try not to complain when I'm at school or work. It would be so easy to call out sick, but I don't. I only missed two classes last academic year. I didn't tell any of the students I taught that I have cancer: I didn't want their sympathy, and I didn't want to make things awkward for myself or them. When I was bald, I'd either wear a headscarf or the same wig on class days because I didn't want to deal with students' questions.

Being accommodating is tricky to navigate. Sometimes I want to tell people, "Fuck off—I'm a cancer patient." Deep down, I'm not that confrontational and you never know what someone else is going through. Sometimes I would just tell my students that I have "bad hands" when I had to ask someone to pop open a roll of film for me or to adjust a tripod. No one ever questioned why I have "bad hands." I didn't look sick, so there was no reason for them to inquire about my health. Notice the past tense there. This semester, I had to drop out of school because I no longer expect to live long enough to graduate. It wouldn't be fair to myself or the students to try to teach when I don't know how much time I have left. I might not make it to Christmas.

It takes everything in me to get off the couch some days. I hate this feeling. This is far removed from the person I was before being diagnosed. I would park as far away from my destination as possible to get in extra steps; I sometimes walked in place to get to my step goal. Now, walking is so painful sometimes, and my fatigue wipes me out. I know that physical activity can help combat fatigue, but what are you supposed to do when you have zero energy—when your feet ache so bad you can barely stand up? It's a vicious, never-ending cycle.

I could try I.V. treatments again, which have fewer side effects—the chemo pump. I fucking hate the pump. I would hear the soft whir of the machine dispensing drugs, even when I wasn't hooked up to it. Sleeping with it was difficult, and carrying it around was cumbersome. I couldn't shower with the pump attached, which was extra miserable in the summer. I finally found a method to bathe with the pump sitting next to the tub, but it was still complicated and uncomfortable.

I wish that I didn't have to endure this. I've stopped wishing that I could get off chemo. I've made peace with being on chemo for life, but that doesn't mean I like it. I have to accept my fate to make it bearable.

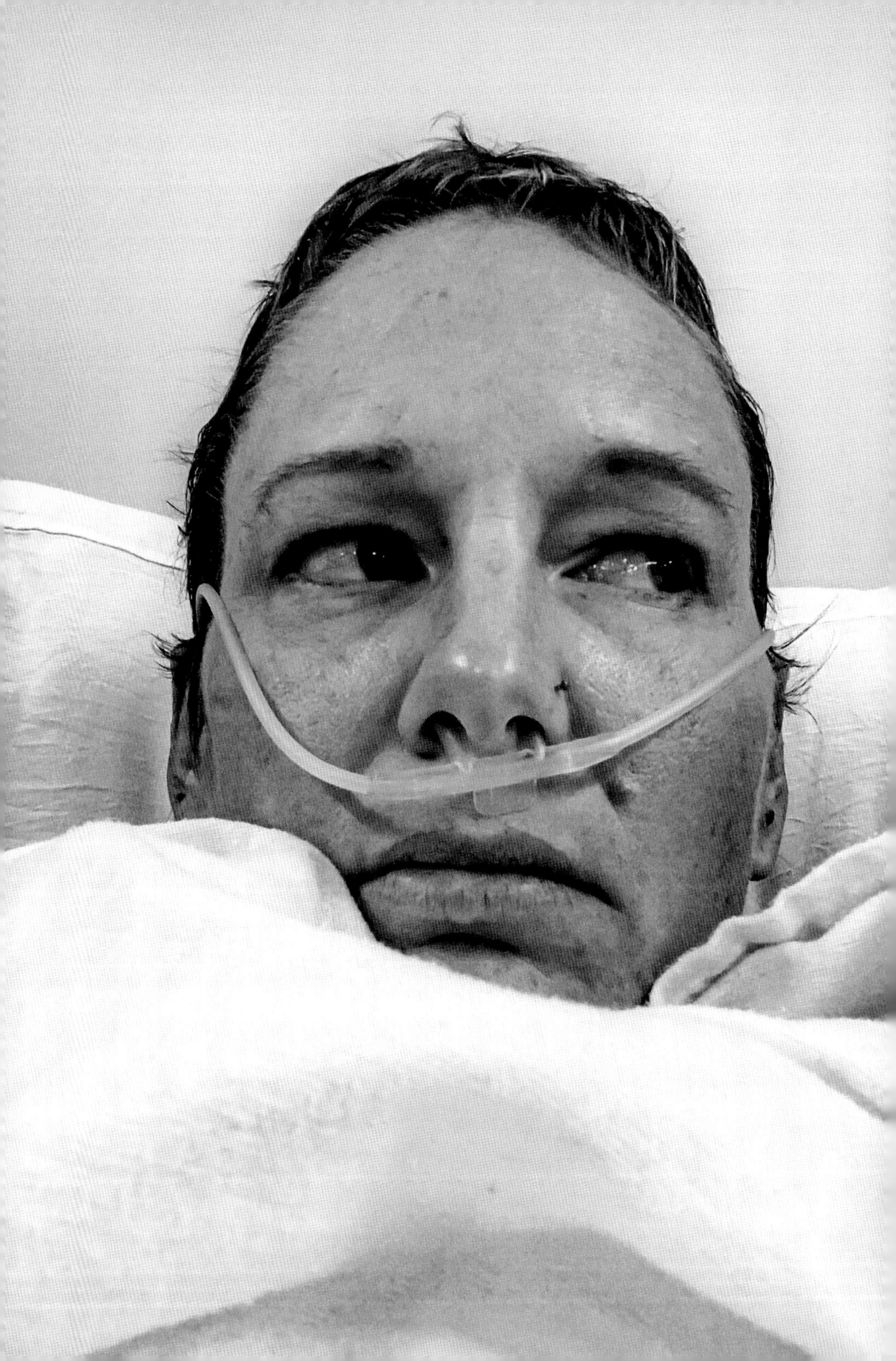

First Descents

My First Descents volunteer trip was intense. First Descents is a nonprofit organization that provides free adventure trips to cancer survivors, their caregivers, and healthcare workers. I was overprepared for my trip in some ways and underprepared in others. I was accepted as the volunteer photographer for a caregiver trip in the Adirondacks in Lake Placid, New York, which I was thrilled about. Back in 2019, I'd attended an FD rock-climbing trip as a participant in Estes Park, Colorado, right after my first year of diagnosis. That first trip was transformative: it was the first time I was surrounded by cancer patients my own age that understood what I was going through. I went rock climbing for the first time. I was challenged both physically and mentally, and I made lifelong friends. After that trip, I knew I wanted to give back to the FD community. I finally got my chance three years later.

The volunteer position is quite different from being a participant. When I went rock climbing myself, that trip was pure magic. FD is so much more than the adventure. I made deep connections with the other cancer survivors. We were fed incredible, healthy meals three times a day and were told the week would be "challenge by choice." We were urged to push ourselves out of our comfort zones, but we weren't forced to do anything that pushed us too far.

FD trips are structured like this: the day starts at 7 a.m. for cold breakfast, 8 a.m. for hot breakfast; you pack your lunch, then pile into three vans at 9 a.m. to go climbing until 5 p.m. You get back to the lodge, then have about an hour and a half until dinner; then, campfire is at 7 p.m. Staff has an hour-long meeting after that, then it is finally bedtime. My experience as staff was fun, deeply rewarding, and incredibly exhausting.

I overestimated my physical limits and was in my head the whole trip, at no fault to anyone else. I wasn't able to rock climb due to my hand and foot syndrome, but I was able to rappel twice, which was great fun. All the climbs required a brief hike through canopied forests. I would normally enjoy these hikes, but my Parinaud Syndrome—a side effect from cancer treatments—made them difficult. I have depth-perception issues since I can't look up and down. The light bounced off the leaves of the trees, which made my vision difficult. The forest floor appeared flat until I was right up on a large rock, or a soft bed of detritus. I needed someone to hold my hand and guide me. I felt like a burden. This trip wasn't supposed to be about me; it was for the participants. I felt a deep sense of guilt, and I was embarrassed that I struggled with an activity that I would normally be good at.

I photographed the participants and other staff members all week, from morning to night. The only break I got was when I went to bed. Even during downtime before dinner, I was culling and editing photos. One day, I edited photos and worked on our end-of-program video for five hours. I didn't mind because the program gave me the opportunity to take candid shots, something I don't get to do much in my regular photography practice. When my vision went south, I had to cancel my commercial work. The FD trip was a good reminder that photography is something that I'm good at and passionate about.

FD trips typically have six staff members: a program lead, an assistant lead, a head chef, a cook, one or two "camp moms," a medic, and a photographer. Our group was down by two people, so staff had to help more than usual. I wasn't sure what was expected of me. I was exhausted and hardly got a moment's rest.

I had zero privacy almost the entire trip. I shared a large room with three other women, and I split a king-sized bed with someone else. I was only by myself for a few hours one day when the cooks were out shopping for that night's dinner. I felt like I had to be *on* at all times. The group was nurturing, but it was still a dynamic that

I'm not used to. I typically spend my days alone at home, unless I have work. I craved the company but also needed my private time. I'd try to sleep in, just to be awakened by everyone else in my room.

I had a breakdown halfway through the trip: it was all too much. I was fatigued, dealing with my vision issues, and I had gastrointestinal problems on top of everything else that I didn't share with anyone besides the medic. One day, I went to the bathroom twenty times. It was mentally and physically taxing. I'm not used to working around the clock like that since I've been on disability for two years and work a hodge-podge of part-time jobs. I was unable to show up as my best self, something I wanted to do for the sake of the participants. I cried to the medic in private, then the lead approached me and I cried again. I was overwhelmed and felt unprofessional because of it.

Mentally, I felt better the next day. I tried to embrace my situation and shed the weight of what I was carrying. I tried to connect more deeply with the participants as a way to distract myself, and I focused even more on my photography.

The last day was my best day. We had a steep yet short hike, and the wall they were climbing was in the shade. One of the guides led me up to the top of the rock wall and roped me in so I could peer over the edge and take photos of the climbers as they ascended. We cheered them on when they got to the top, and my vantage point provided a unique perspective. A breeze made it cooler and clearer than below.

Despite the trip's challenges, if given the chance I would volunteer again. The experience was rewarding, and I think I would have a much better time now that I know what to expect. It meant a lot to lend my talents to a community that I feel passionately about, and it felt good to give rather than take, even as a cancer patient in active treatment.

Thomas went on a caregiver trip two months after my volunteer trip. He went white-water kayaking in Oregon on the Rogue River. I'd suggested that he take a caregiver trip two years ago, but COVID screwed everything up. He was finally on his trip when I learned about my terminal LMD diagnosis. We'd already received grim brain MRI results the week before from my neurosurgeon, but the week he was gone was when my oncologist and radiologist spelled everything out for me. I waited to tell Thomas the news until he returned home. I didn't want to ruin what he would later describe to me as "one of the best things I've ever done in my life."

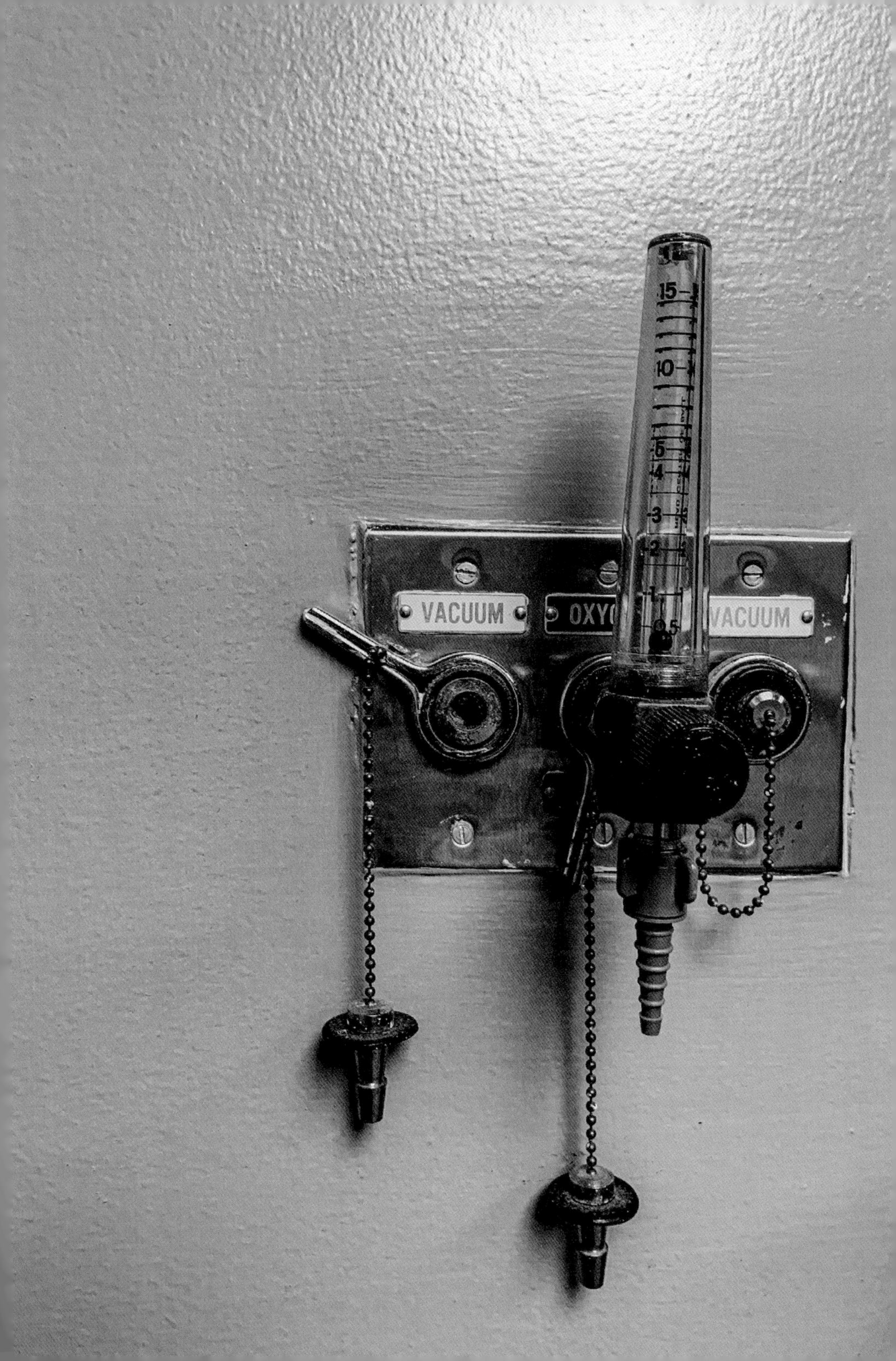
VACUUM
VACUUM
15
10
5
4
3
2
1
0.5

Lifespan

The lifespan of a house finch is three to five years. The life expectancy of a stage-IV colorectal cancer patient is unknown, but there is only a 15 percent chance for stage-IV patients to make it to the five-year mark. I was diagnosed four years ago, long before the finches set up house in my front porch light fixture. This is the third set of baby birds we've had. Several years ago, when I was younger and healthier, a momma and papa bird built a nest. We never took it down, and last year, we were delighted to discover three baby birds were growing in their home. It takes two to three weeks for the babies to grow strong enough to fly out of the nest. We were hoping for three weeks, but they left at two. This summer, a third set of birds used our light fixture.

There's a sweet olive tree in our front yard, where our old landlord's ashes are buried underneath. We're the landlords now, so all the responsibility lies on us. Cat claw has engulfed the tree. Every year I fight the cat claw, trying to whack down the invasive vine but never able to grab it by its roots—much like the efforts my oncologist makes to beat down my cancer. My tumors have been stable, but I'm never sure when they're going to take over my body, choking out my healthy cells. For now, the cancer is contained to my lungs and brain. It's cold comfort to be thankful for the cancer not spreading to other organs yet, especially in light of my new diagnosis.

Eventually, I gave up on the cat claw and let nature take its course. Now, it's difficult to tell where the tree starts and the cat claw ends. We've deemed the tree The Bird Hotel. The extra coverage from the vines provides privacy for the birds, which you can hear all day long—especially in the mornings and evenings. I imagine they are sharing hot neighborhood gossip, maybe talking smack about the murder of crows that occasionally descends on our neighborhood like bored teenagers, or the blue jay that nibbles on my feral cat's food on the back porch.

I looked like a baby bird when my hair was growing back in from chemo. I lost my hair three times. I hoped for a smooth, even buzzcut. What I got was a patch of hair here, a patch of hair there. I felt vulnerable, like I wasn't ready for the world. Now that I have a full head of hair again, I blend in, camouflaged like a healthy person. But I'm far, far from that. When I start full brain radiation in a few weeks, my hair will fall out for a fourth time. I probably won't live long enough to watch it grow back.

I recently developed Parinaud Syndrome, a condition brought on from radiation to a brain tumor that was found this past January. It started as double vision, and now everything is blurry and I've lost the ability to look up and down. Bright light affects me as well, and I am unable to fully close my eyelids. My doctors assured me that my condition is temporary. I feel so fragile every time I leave my house. I can see, but I can't see well. I wonder what those baby finches see as they peer out their nest, grappling at making sense of the big world out there from the cozy confines of a bed of well-worn twigs. I've taken to wearing my eye patch again: it's the only way I can see normally.

I've been sleeping more than usual. Maybe it's the summer heat that crept in early; maybe it's the bone-deep fatigue that comes with being on chemo off and on (mostly on) for four years. The babies look so vulnerable. Their tiny heads are gray as they wait for their feathers to grow in—a patch here, a patch there. Their yellow beaks are open, ready to receive whatever nourishment Mom brings them. I am open to whatever miracles may come my way.

Just like last summer, the baby finches have been a joy to watch. I get excited every time I see a tiny beak peeking out, mouth wide. Unlike last summer's occupants, the male hasn't been around as much. It seems like the mother is shouldering all the responsibility.

I've noticed a decrease in friends checking up on me. If I look fine then I must be fine, right? Just because my tumors are stable doesn't mean I'm fine. Then, when I learned about my new terminal diagnosis, I received an influx of support. I don't want to sound ungrateful, but where were all these people just a month ago?

Soon, those baby finches will fly away. They probably won't go far. I bet they'll take up residence in The Bird Hotel again. It will be impossible to distinguish them from the other occupants. Still, I won't forget them. It's incredible how something so simple and sweet leaves a mark on us. I check on the babies every day, delighting in seeing their tiny heads peeking out the nest. I'm bad at asking for what I need. Unlike those babies, I try not to be a burden on anyone. Fortunately, the birds don't have an awareness like that. There's no need for apologies for needing care. Maybe I should reach out to my friends more often.

The difference between those birds and me is time and unawareness. We won't have to watch them die, even though their lifespan is relatively short. We won't know when they're gone. I won't outlive those finches. I hate thinking about what will happen at the end of my life. I try not to play out scenarios in my head. Still, I get sad when I think about how much I will be missed.

One morning, my husband and I witnessed a baby flying out of the nest. Its newly formed feathers distinguished it as ready to go, much like a plucky high schooler ready to graduate and strike out on their own. We watched the bird stand on the edge of the light fixture, unsure of itself. Then, after a few seconds of hesitation, it took flight for the first time. We delighted in watching it, so proud of our baby but also sad that we wouldn't be able to watch its growth anymore.

A few months later, we were in Sedona, Arizona, for the third summer in a row. We rented the same apartment we always do. A highway separates us from the mountain preserve across from the apartment. There is plenty of space for birds, but a momma decided to build a nest in a decorative metal sun on the front of the building. When we arrived, there were four babies in the nest, all patchy heads and tiny beaks. Just like back home, Mom and Dad perched on a power line closest to the nest. I could hear the familiar, frantic high-pitched chirp of babies getting fed. Of all the places to build a nest, why there? I took it as a good sign, a symbol of a life going on.

It took less than a week for the babies to take flight. I was happy for them, growing so big and strong. But I also mourned my loss. Is this what it is like when your kid goes off to college? I'll never see these birds again. We'll be back home in a few days, wondering whatever happened to those finches. I hope they found the nature preserve. I hope they eat as many big, fat bugs as they can and live out their lives to old age.

I want to be remembered, just like those birds.

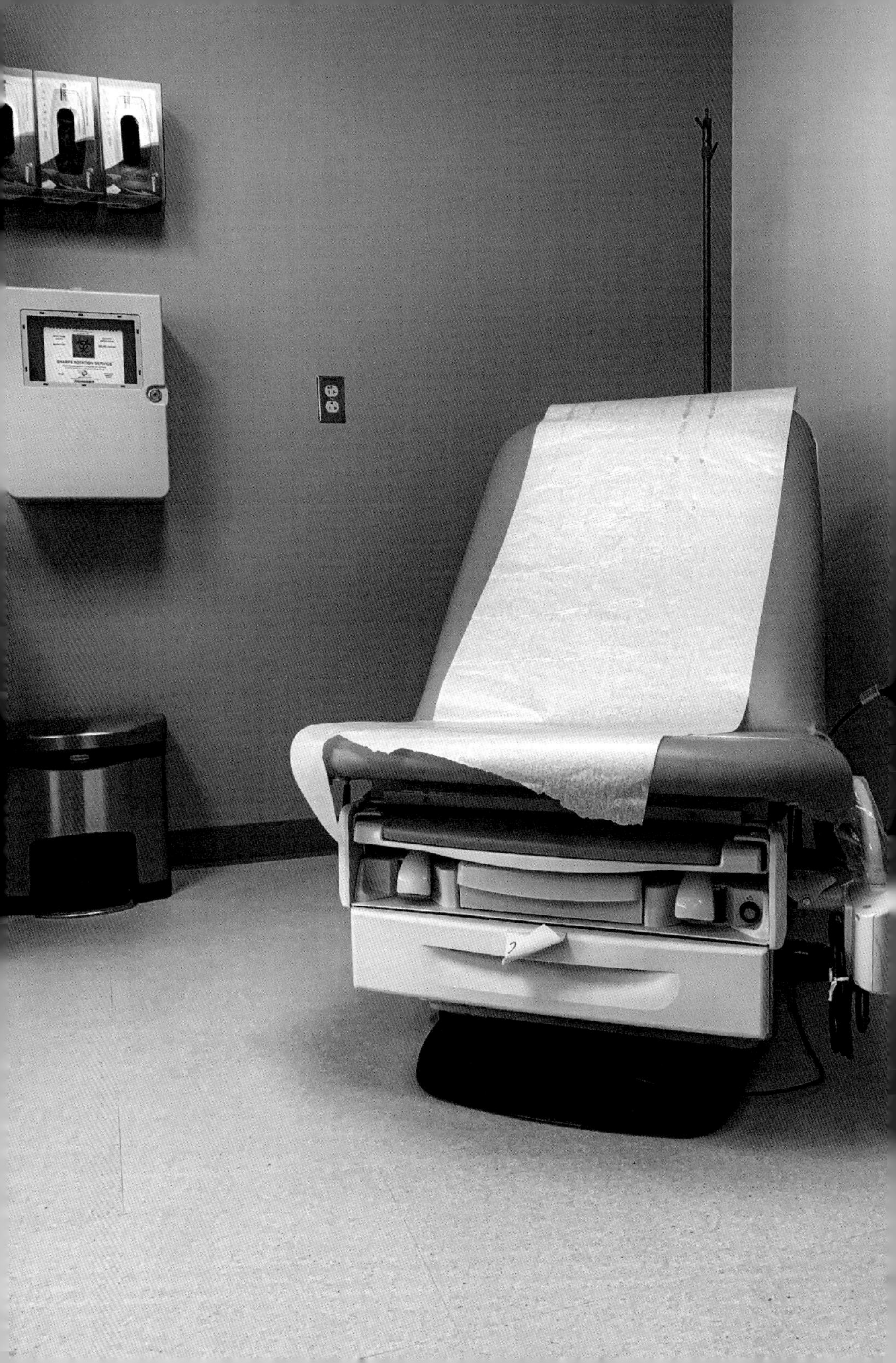
SHARPS ROTATION SERVICE

On Joy

I desperately strive for joy. I took up roller skating again during my first year of cancer treatment. I've skated off and on all my life. I had my thirteenth birthday at the roller-skating rink. In college I would sometimes skate on the lakefront, whizzing down the hilly parts.

New Orleans' own Jon Batiste said joy is always accessible to us, even during our darkest moments. Joy is a mindset, not just something that happens to us. We have to choose joy, no matter what we're going through. It's easy to let the dark moments shadow everything we do. I firmly believe that I must embrace my reality instead of trying to fight it. That doesn't mean I'm happy about my medical situation, but I can't let it ruin my life any more than it has. There is something incredibly rewarding about taking back your power. It's also one of the most difficult things I have ever done.

Joy doesn't have to be a grandiose statement. I find joy in both the little and big things. I love sitting on my front porch and listening to the birds sing as I admire our garden. I appreciate kind gestures. I get much joy in spending time with my niece, having a good meal, fresh sheets on the bed—any little thing I can. I get much of my joy from being in nature.

I don't believe in forced joy. Toxic positivity is a real thing. Many people think if they just remain positive then bad things won't happen to them—or they choose to ignore them. For me, the most joy I get is when I'm doing physical activities, like hiking, roller skating, or rock climbing. I used to run three times a week. I was consistently running in the top 10 percent in 5K races for my age group prior to my diagnosis. I wasn't super fast, but I was proud of my relative speed considering I had never been a runner before.

Now, it's becoming increasingly harder to stay in shape. I'm not sure if it's mental, physical, or both. I'm feeling more fragile than I am. The intense summer heat doesn't help. When it feels like 105 degrees outside, it's hard for anyone to function, much less people like me. Intense heat can turn deadly too fast. Thomas and I have been swimming two to three times a week at the public natatorium for the past year. I find great joy in swimming—feeling the weightlessness of my body while swimming laps—or in the sense of community when we do an aqua fitness class.

I find so much joy in photography. It feels good to be paid for something I'm good at. The money is nice, but it's more than that. Money is the tangible thing for putting value on my work. It's validating when someone values your efforts. And after putting in years of practice, it's good to see how my work has improved considerably.

Other little joys include a good meal, a great song, the way my dog gets excited to see me when I return from a trip. I get so frustrated about not being able to do the physical activities I used to. Part of that is the summer: it is scorching hot in New Orleans. Imagine someone throwing a hot, wet wool blanket on your head. Now, imagine taking off the blanket and having someone blow you in the face with a blow dryer. I'm off work all summer long, and I can't drive right now because of my vision issues, which means I'm often sequestered indoors. I've been sleeping far more than I care to admit. Part of me feels lazy; part of me knows that this is my body telling me to slow down and rest. I hate sleeping so late. It robs me of my days.

After Hurricane Ida last year, I walked around our neighborhood with my camera. I came upon a lilliputian scene in the crook of an oak tree's roots. Someone had nestled a tiny flamingo, along with a scattering of marbles, in the tree. After the city had experienced so much damage—power outages, festering trash on the sidewalks, roofs ripped off homes—that diorama provided me with a glimpse of joy and hope. I photographed it and left it untouched for the next person to enjoy.

Food brings me joy when it is very, very good. It doesn't have to be an expensive meal, just fun or delicious (or both). Some of my fondest memories are sitting around, breaking bread with good friends or family. My brother's Thanksgiving meals are the stuff of legends—everything made from scratch and love. Before my brother moved back to New Orleans, Thomas and I would drive up to Louisville, Kentucky, to partake in his epic feasts. We would sit around together all day and nosh from sun up to sun down.

Seeing my niece, either in person or through a phone screen, is a big joy for me. She's three years old, and it's delightful to watch her vocabulary grow. Just a few days ago, my sister had me on speaker phone and Hazel yelled, "Christy, I tooted!" She's also taken a liking to the phrase "Guess what? Chicken butt!" I desperately want to live long enough to see her grow up, but I know that I won't be around long enough for her first high school dance. A part of me feels guilty; I'll probably be her first funeral. I don't want to make anyone sad. It's a hard place to be. I just hope I help give Hazel as much joy in her life as she deserves.

As depressing as an inevitable early death is, I manage to find a lot of joy in life that I would otherwise take for granted. I wouldn't say cancer has been a gift, but it has made me appreciate the little things that I thought were a given. It's cliche, but true: I'm now savoring every second of life. Nothing in this life is a given. I was the unfortunate one to find out.

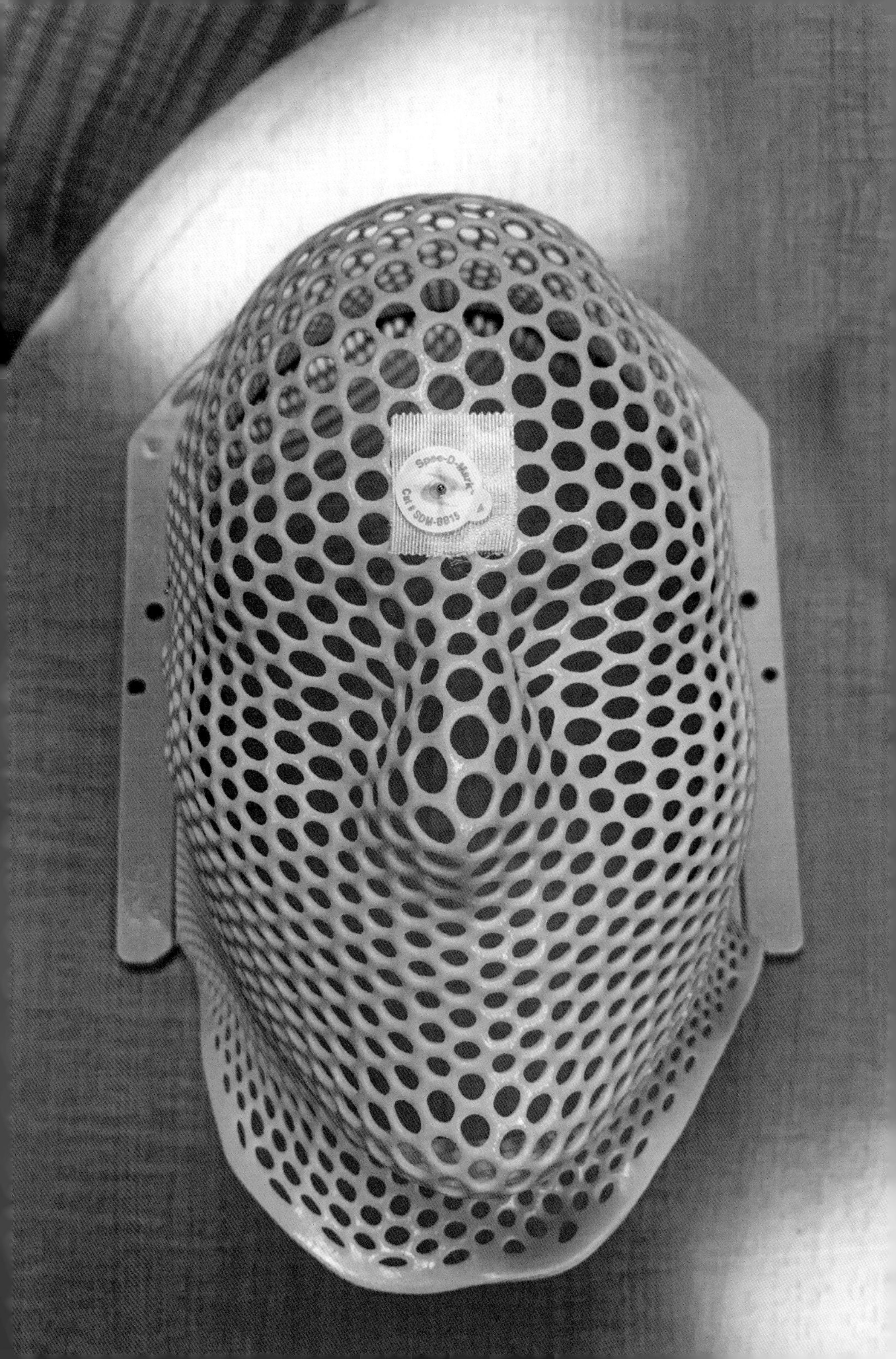
Cat # SDM-BB15

On Loneliness

There is a loneliness that comes with cancer treatment, especially at a young age. I was thirty-eight when I was diagnosed. I didn't know a single person my age with cancer. I do have an incredible support system; my mom and brother-in-law drove me to treatment sessions. When I had my first surgery, a craniotomy, my sister and her husband flew here to be with me. Through everything, Thomas has been a nonstop caregiver. Still, going to treatment that first year of my diagnosis was alienating and lonely. People can empathize, but it's a much different experience when it's happening to you.

While I was working on my first master's degree, I would sit at my campus job, so weak that I could barely hobble across the street to grab lunch. In class, my chemo pump would make sounds as it dispensed poison into me. An I.V. line inserted into my chest was tethered to my pump, contained in what looked like a black fanny pack. I tried to hide as much of my I.V. line as I could, yet it would inevitably creep out of my shirt. I would nod off in class sometimes, not because I was bored but because I simply didn't have the energy.

My bald head was the only indicator that I was sick. It took a few months for me to muster the courage to go out in public without my head wrapped in a scarf. When I did, students were startled as I passed them in the hallways. I've lost my hair three times because of cancer treatment. It's dreadful seeing your hair floating in the bathtub. Fistfuls of hair would cover my pillow every night. I mourned the loss of my hair. I could easily moonlight as a healthy person when I had hair. Whether I had hair or not, it was the first time that I would stand in a crowd of people and feel alone. It was as if I was the only person in the world going through cancer treatment.

A few weeks before the first semester after I was diagnosed began, I went to a dinner party at a classmate's house. I had just undergone brain surgery and my chest port was placed, ready to accept chemo. I talked with a noticeable slur, a side effect from the craniotomy. Only two of my classmates knew I had cancer. I wasn't ready to make an announcement, and I hoped people wouldn't notice my slur. But it was hard not to. When I was leaving, a friend who knew about my cancer leaned in for a hug. I told her to hug me only from the left side as my port was still sore from surgery. One of my nosy classmates butted in and asked why. I knew she was suspicious that something was wrong with me by the way she was acting toward me. I blurted out "I have cancer" and her eyes widened. She clearly wasn't expecting that answer.

It's exhausting to rehash all of my experiences and explain medical terms to people—what a PET scan is, my side effects, any new diagnosis. Most people who aren't terminally ill have a hard time realizing how terrifying it is to face your own mortality on a daily basis. I get it. I didn't have a clue about any of this, even though I've had multiple family members die from cancer. It's unpleasant. It's uncomfortable. But it's something I have to face.

After my first year of treatment, I went on three different cancer trips. The first two were for young adults; the second one was a colorectal cancer conference. It felt good to be around people who get it, especially people in my age group. I've made some lifelong friends who also have cancer—people I wouldn't have met otherwise. It's the unofficial club that no one wants to be a part of, but we're all glad that we have each other.

I never wonder what my life would be like if I didn't have a terminal illness. It's not worth the grief that that would cause. And yet it's frustrating being a graduate student. Until a few weeks ago, I was working on my second master's degree. I dropped out when I found out about my new diagnosis. While my cohort was excited about what their future careers may look like, I'd hoped to live long enough to graduate.

I see job opportunities that would be a dream to take, but I can't work full time. Hell, I can't even work part time. I do freelance work, which provides me with sporadic paychecks. I couldn't commit to a regular job because I never know how I'm going to feel. My ongoing vision problems would make it difficult to maintain work commitments. A friend of mine, someone I met at cancer camp, recently went blind. I was horrified that I might go blind as well. My vision issues are probably temporary, but it's still hard to function in everyday life. When my sight first went bad three months ago, I was scared as I tried to navigate the world in a new way. Just walking from my house to return a library book by myself was petrifying. That activity normally wouldn't faze me. Crime has increased significantly in New Orleans over the summer, and I worried that if someone tried to jump me I wouldn't have any defenses. I wouldn't be able to clearly see what was happening.

I try my best not to dominate conversations with going on and on about my suffering. No one wants to hear that—not really. Right before my grandma died three years ago, she fixated on her medical issues. My family knew better than to ask her how she was doing. I tried to explain to her that obsessing over her health wasn't doing her any good. She died of a heart attack a few weeks after I had surgery. I only cried once, not because I wasn't upset. I was too overwhelmed with my own bullshit to take on any more.

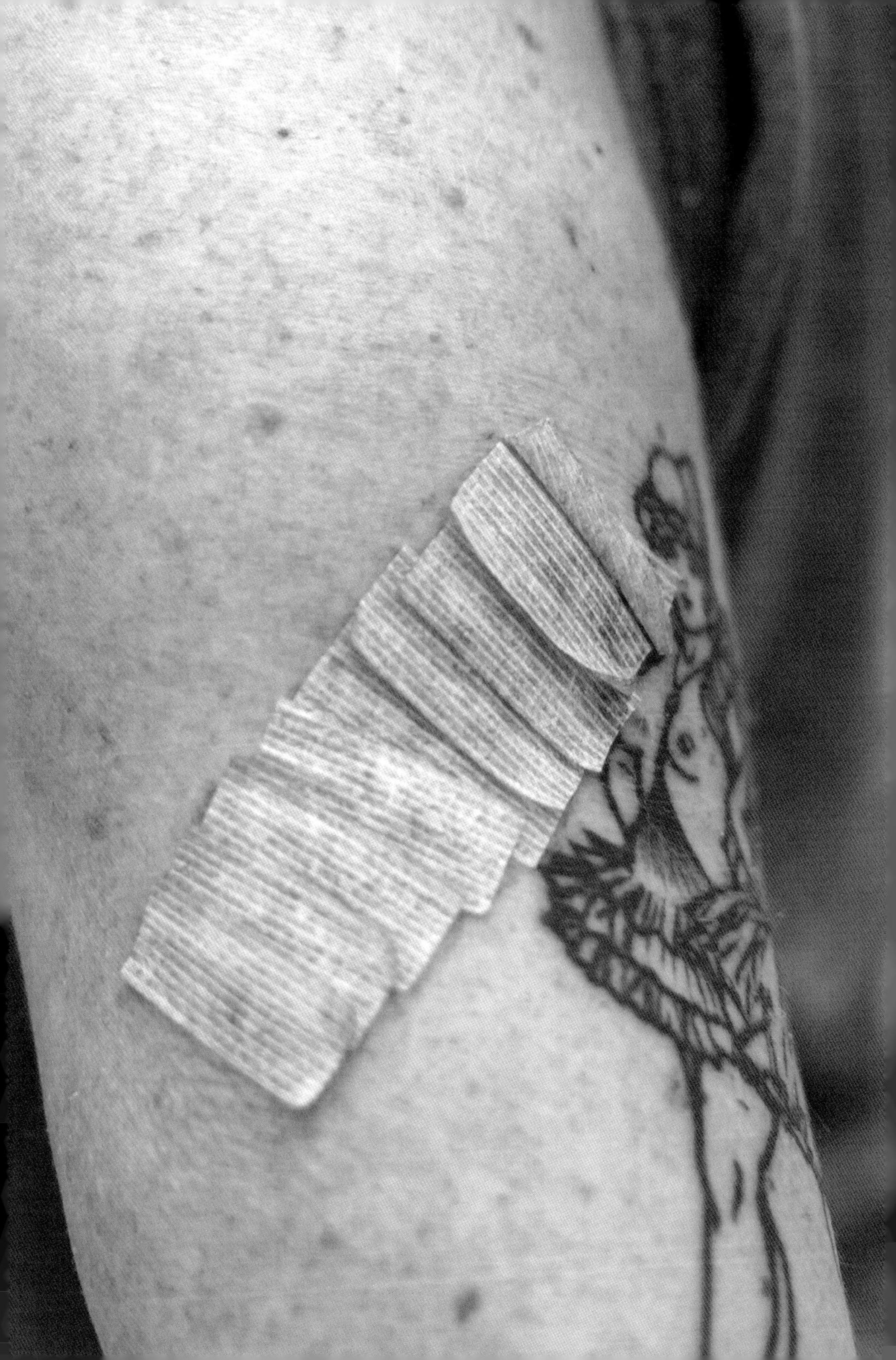

Scars

I DON'T CARE about scars anymore. After all I've been through, scars are the least of my concerns. A few years before my first diagnosis, Thomas and I went on a summer trip to San Marcos, Texas. I banged my knee up on a rock at a popular swimming hole. There was blood everywhere, and I had a nasty gash, one that left me with a sizable scar. When we came back home, I bought a scar cream loaded with vitamin E. The scar went away, which thrilled me at the time. In hindsight, I doubt anyone would have even noticed it.

I was a pretty adventurous kid, a tomboy. I played with dolls but I also went fishing with my dad, climbed trees—things like that. I would get the occasional scrape or bruise but nothing serious. It wasn't until I was diagnosed with cancer that the scars started racking up, like sick trophies.

My first scar—and the first surgery of my life—was a craniotomy. My neurosurgeon sliced my scalp open, revealing my skull as he removed my tumor. I was left with a sliver of missing hair. It was only when my hair fell out from chemo that the scar was visible, a line where I was cut open. I can feel the scar tissue when I run my hand over my head, a slight bump that I'd rather not touch.

My biggest scars were from my lower anterior resection, when my colorectal surgeon removed my rectum and the rectal tumor through a laparoscopic procedure. Two scars on my abdomen have since disappeared and a line cuts through my pubic bone, like a smaller version of a C-section scar. My sister gave birth to my niece a week before my surgery, and we would complain to each other about the pain we were both in. My scar has faded over time, just a faint memento of that five-hour operation.

My stoma, a nub of my small intestines that stuck out my stomach, is the biggest scar. I pooped out of my stomach for nine weeks as my rectum healed. An adhesive bag collected the feces, which I do not miss at all. My reversal surgery was quick. It took about an hour and left me with a gaping hole, which slowly healed as my skin grew over it. There is a divot and a scar where my stoma once was, which is only visible when I wear a low-cut bikini.

They aren't scars, but my body is littered with five tiny blue tattoos: symbols of radiation. I have two on each thigh and three on my chest. Radiation is painless, but it does have long-lasting consequences. My pelvic radiation sent me into early menopause, and my lung radiation left me with a cough and shortness of breath. The latter is slowly improving, but radiation has affected me in ways I couldn't have imagined. I've had gamma knife three times, which is radiation surgery to treat brain tumors. Gamma knife is target therapy, whereas full brain radiation radiates the entire brain. I'm about to endure the latter, which will temporarily wipe out my short-term memory.

As if having stage-IV rectal cancer isn't bad enough, I had a bout of melanoma two years ago. My dermatologist said it was most likely from sun exposure I had as a kid. The large, brown mole developed next to a pinup tattoo of two women in costumes on the back of my left arm. Fortunately, we caught it at the stage-0 phase and my melanoma was noninvasive. My dermatological surgeon excised the mole and the surrounding tissue, getting close to my girls but not enough to shave off a foot or part of a leg. I have an indent in my arm and a long line of a scar. I had two other skin biopsies—one on my right arm, one on my left buttock—for suspicious moles. When my dermatologist apologized for the scar on my butt I laughed it off: "A scar is the last thing I'm worried about."

Physical scars are nothing compared to mental scars. I live my life scan to scan, hoping for the best every three months. I have a PET scan, which detects cancer in the body. I have brain MRIs. I see both my dermatologist and my colorectal surgeon every six months. I have blood work and see my oncologist every other week. Keeping up with my medical schedule is exhausting.

I try not to dwell on these things. No good comes from me stewing in misery. I've tried to minimize cancer as much as I can. People tell me that I'm an inspiration and that I'm strong and brave, but I don't see myself that way. I don't have a choice in the matter. It's either this or die. I want to live, and I want to live fully. I can still do most of the things that I loved to do prediagnosis. Instead of focusing on what I can't do, I try to focus on what I can do. I can still swim; I can still go to the gym. I can still roller skate (when my vision clears up). I can still laugh and cry when I need to. I can still FaceTime with my niece; I can still walk the dogs. I can still be me, at least for now.

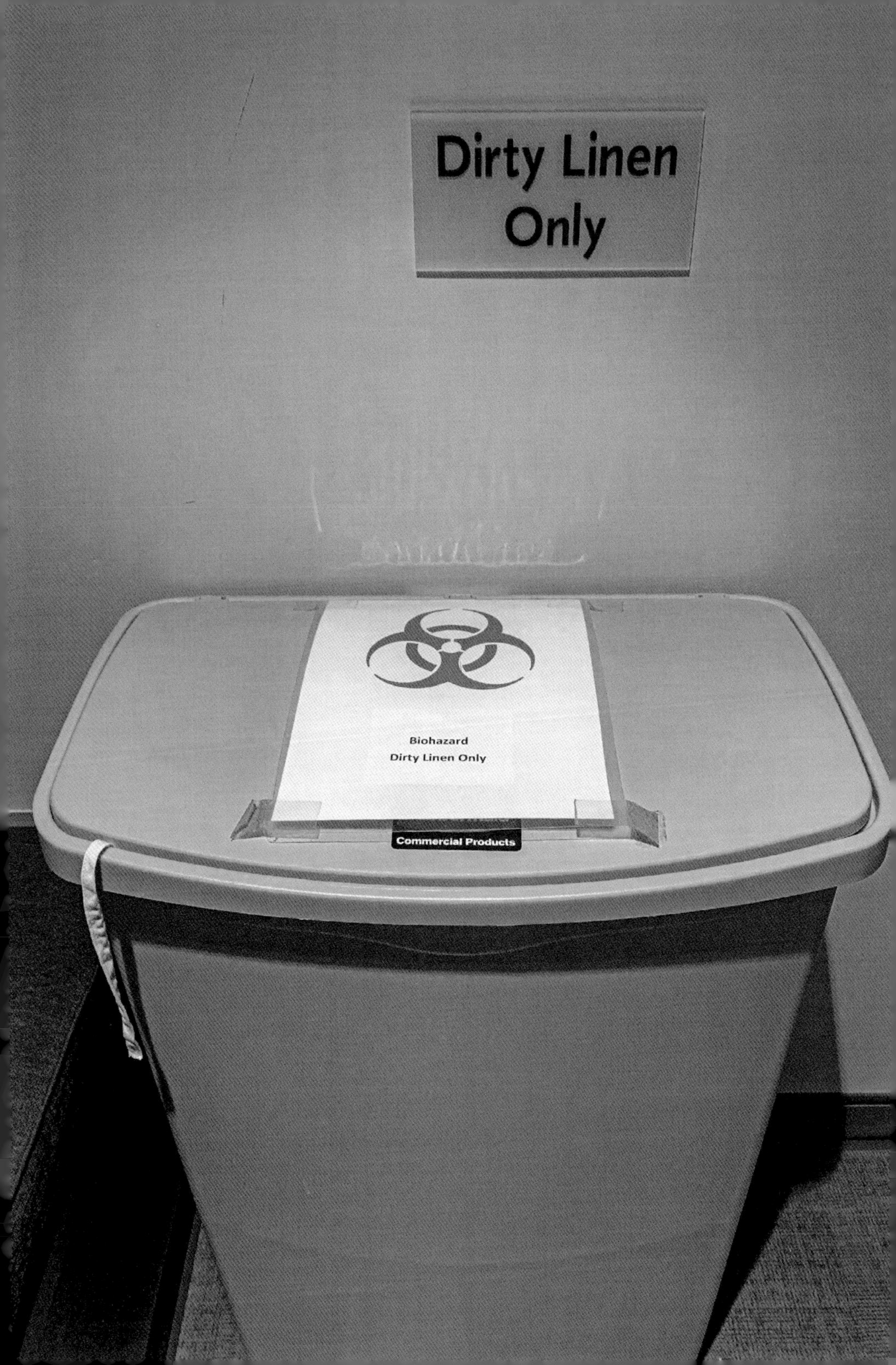
Dirty Linen
Only
Biohazard
Dirty Linen Only
Commercial Products

Shitty Situation

Everyone poops, but things are a little different when you don't have a rectum. I had a tumor in my butt, which was removed during a procedure called Lower Anterior Resection, which causes Lower Anterior Resection Syndrome, or LARS for short. My colorectal surgeon removed my entire rectum to prevent my cancer from returning to the same spot, which was the origin of my cancer.

I was fortunate that I didn't need a permanent ostomy bag thanks to the location of my tumor, which was high up enough that I didn't lose complete control of my bowels. Instead, I got a J-pouch. My surgeon made a new poop receptacle out of my small intestines. While it doesn't function like my original plumbing, it ensures that I can go to the bathroom like normal. Think of a J-pouch like two open-ended sausages sitting side by side. The stool collects inside, similar to a rectum. However, the small intestines don't have the same nerve endings as a rectum. Once poop gets inside, there's an immediate urge to go to the bathroom. It's also harder to pass stool: think of pushing clay down a straw.

There is so much that we take for granted when it comes to our bodies. Before cancer, I never thought much of my internal organs. They were fully functional. Now, I'm acutely aware of my bottom. When nature calls, it's a stressful situation. Will I make it to the bathroom in time? Will chemo give me diarrhea? If I'm in a public place, I sometimes worry about taking too long. I used to get frustrated when people took a long time in the bathroom. Now I understand that sometimes it's not possible to get your business done quickly.

There's also the frequency. If I don't give myself an enema, I often have to go multiple times to get out one bowel movement—up to twenty times a day. Pooping that much hurts. I once had to ice down my butthole just to get some relief. It's all very embarrassing.

My body's mechanics make me feel broken, like a car that won't start right away.

Public outings aren't a source of stress for me, unless I have difficulty finding a bathroom. Last summer, I went on an overnight camping trip in Arizona. West Fork is a beautiful hike, with an easy first few miles down into a canyon under a veil of trees. Once the trail ends, you wade through a creek in order to get to your campsite. We didn't make it to the official campsite. I fell in the water twice, banging my knee against the rocks. We decided to turn around and set up camp on a sandy embankment instead. That night, I had to go. I popped a squat, which felt like the most natural thing. My body felt at ease, which made me wonder why our western toilets are designed the way they are. A pelvic floor therapist told me to get a squatty potty, which makes it easier to go. She was right.

I'm an open book when it comes to sharing my cancer experience, but talking about poop makes me uncomfortable. There are things I am holding back even here, despite advocating for others to be comfortable discussing their basic bodily functions. There are some things that I need to hold close, to avoid giving away my entire medical history and ailments. So much of cancer treatment strips me of my dignity. I often joke that I've had more cameras up my butt than most porn stars. Every six months my colorectal surgeon sends a scope up my butt to check my J-pouch and look for any new tumors. I've been tumor-free since my initial round of chemo, at least in my butt. Unfortunately, I can't say the same for my brain, lungs, and lymph nodes.

There's such a stigma associated with pooping. Everyone does it, yet no one wants to talk about it. Look, I get it. I didn't want to talk about it either, which is the problem with why people get colorectal cancer in the first place. That said, I didn't have symptoms before

I was initially diagnosed. A lot of the symptoms, such as bloating, can be attributable to so many other things, like menstruation.

Imagine this: you grab a packet of honey out of the fridge, one of those single-serve packets you find at a coffee shop. You rip a sliver into the top corner. You squeeze the honey out. It comes out slowly as you put pressure on it to eke out every last drop. The honey comes out in spurts. You get frustrated that it's taking so long. You keep squeezing until you think the packet is empty, but a little drop comes out every time. This is what pooping with LARS is like. It's an ordeal—one that can wreck your entire day and cause intense pain.

Sometimes I take Imodium to give myself a break, but it's often not worth it. I'm just delaying the inevitable. It's miserable, but I don't have it as bad as some people. In one private Facebook group I'm in, people complain about pooping themselves, or they live with chronic pain. They're afraid to eat certain foods, ranging from dairy to bell peppers, because they believe certain foods trigger their LARS. I eat whatever I want and have found ways to cope and manage my body. But sometimes my body wins. Sometimes I wake up with shit in my underwear. Not often, but it happens. I can't believe I'm sharing all of this. It's humiliating, even when I don't tell people. I'm embarrassed for myself, utterly degraded by my own body.

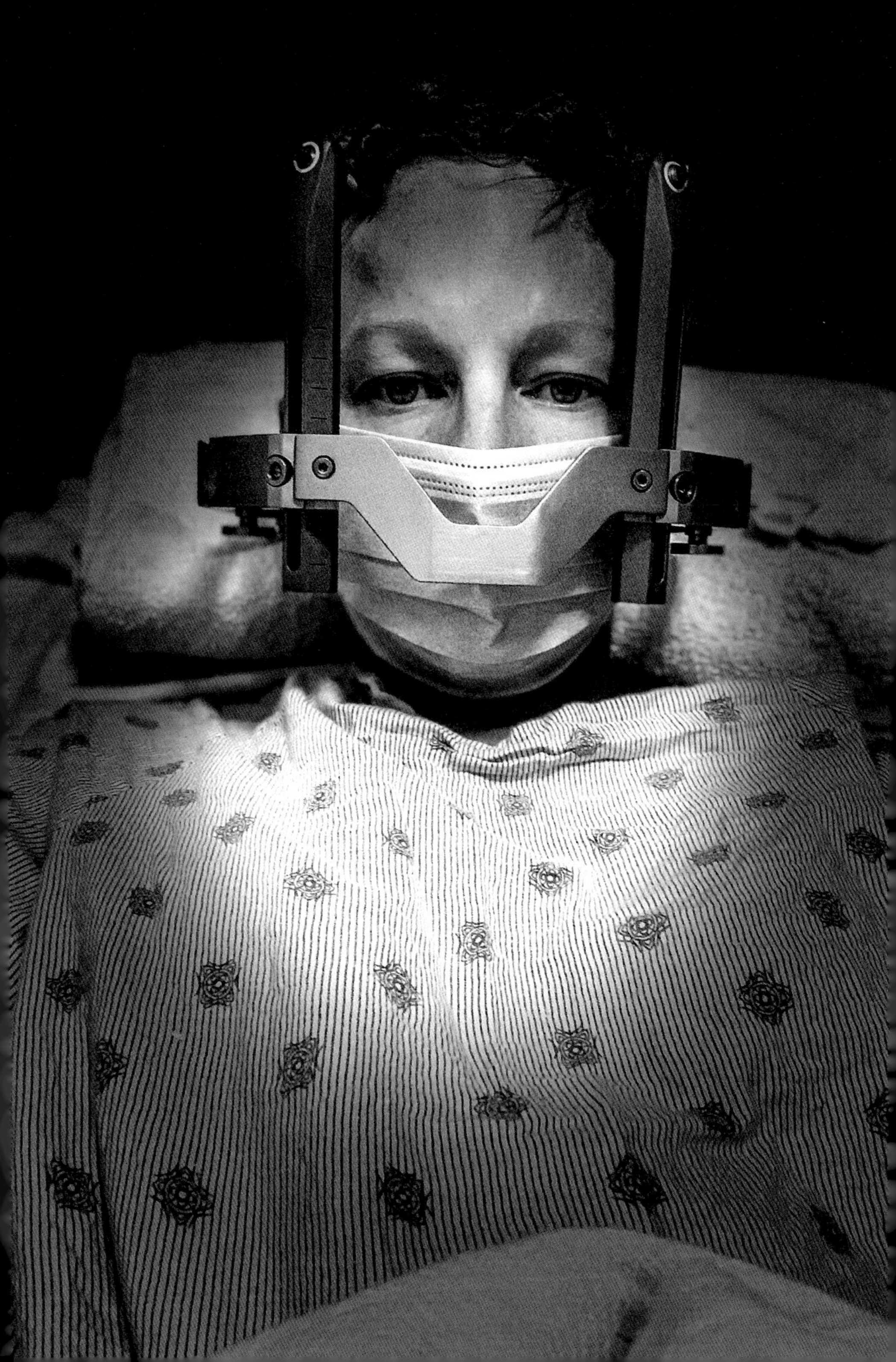

Staying Alive

Staying alive is a full-time job. I knew I was stage-IV upon my initial diagnosis, but I didn't know what that entailed. I thought that stage-IV was an immediate death sentence. As time has passed, I realize that I will die from cancer. I've been on chemo for most of the past four years; the longest break I had was six months. Those six months should have felt like a dream. Instead, they were some of the more stressful times, at least initially.

Being a survivor and not a patient felt like purgatory. I suddenly didn't know who I was anymore. I didn't have cancer (or so I thought) and I was done with treatment—at least at that time. Lots of survivors go through the same thing I did. I had a breakdown, an identity crisis. No one told me what to expect. In hindsight, I shouldn't be surprised. I got over that period by returning to Ireland. At first, I was thrilled to go back and get the summer I deserved. But as the date approached, I was terrified. I was returning to a place where I had no support system—where my worst nightmare manifested. A few days before, I told Thomas and several friends that I didn't know if I could get on that plane. When it came time to go to the airport, something in me snapped. I wasn't going to let my fears spoil this trip. It ended up being very cathartic, a way to get back a little piece of me.

The cancer came back and spread to my lungs pretty quickly. I did extensive traveling that summer: six weeks in Ireland, then three weeks on cancer trips. I knew I had lung nodules before I went, but my oncologist said they were too small to biopsy and to enjoy my summer. We had a mold issue in our house, so I hoped that was the cause. When I had my next scan, the nodules had grown. A lung biopsy confirmed that it was cancer.

Back in the infusion chair, I did another ten months of chemo, and five rounds of radiation. I hoped this would do the trick. During that time, COVID lockdown happened, which tarnished graduating with my first masters degree. I enrolled in a second masters program for the following academic year. Thomas and I also decided to spend six weeks in Sedona. With the pandemic in full effect, health insurance companies started to cover telehealth. He's a licensed counselor and could now work from anywhere. We'd dreamed of spending summers in Arizona for years, and here was our chance. We booked an apartment for a month the first chance we got.

I finished lung radiation a few weeks before our trip. Again, it was a similar situation. I moved into the "wait and see" phase of my treatment. When I came back, I found out the tumor was still there, and I now had two new, smaller ones as well. I switched oncologists and learned I'd be on chemo for life, which was my new worst nightmare. Then I learned I also had melanoma and a brain tumor recurrence. I knew things were bad when my psychologist called to check up on me—something she had never done before.

My heart rate started to skyrocket and I'd lose my breath for no immediately clear reason. I took an EKG and my heart was fine. Stress and side effects from radiation were the culprits. Somehow, I got through it all as I was starting my first semester in a new grad program. It was difficult but I soldiered on, pouring my energy into school. I've found school to be a good distraction, a reason to get up in the morning.

I don't keep tabs on the numbers, but I'm approaching one hundred rounds of chemo. I've noticed the longer I'm doing this, the harder it gets on my body. I try to exercise as much as I can. My concentration is shit. I skim news articles instead of reading them in full. I have a hard time reading books, so I just stopped, something that I miss. My memory was awful for a long time, but it's improved a bit.

Then there are the countless doctor appointments. I have lab work and my oncology visits every other week, which aligns with my chemo schedule. I have a weak vocal cord thanks to a cancer-riddled lymph node resting on my right vocal cord. My voice is raspy sometimes, and I started speech therapy to correct it. My eyesight was affected by brain radiation, which was close to my pineal gland. I have skin checks once every six months to make sure my melanoma hasn't come back. I have brain MRIs and PET scans once every three months, and I see my colorectal surgeon once every six months. And that's not including my primary care physician, my OB/GYN, my ophthalmologist: the list goes on.

I haven't been to the dentist in two years. I went right after Hurricane Zeta hit New Orleans. We still didn't have power, but the dental office was running on generators. I cried at the dentist. When you're constantly undergoing invasive procedures, even the tiniest thing will set you off. I told the hygienist I had cancer. Chemo is hard on your teeth, and I expected the worst. Fortunately my teeth were in good shape, but the experience was traumatizing.

My phone is my lifeline. If I don't put every appointment into my calendar, I tend to forget it. I can barely keep up with all of my appointments. There are so many moving parts, so many medications I'm on. It's a lot, and the longer I'm alive the harder it gets.

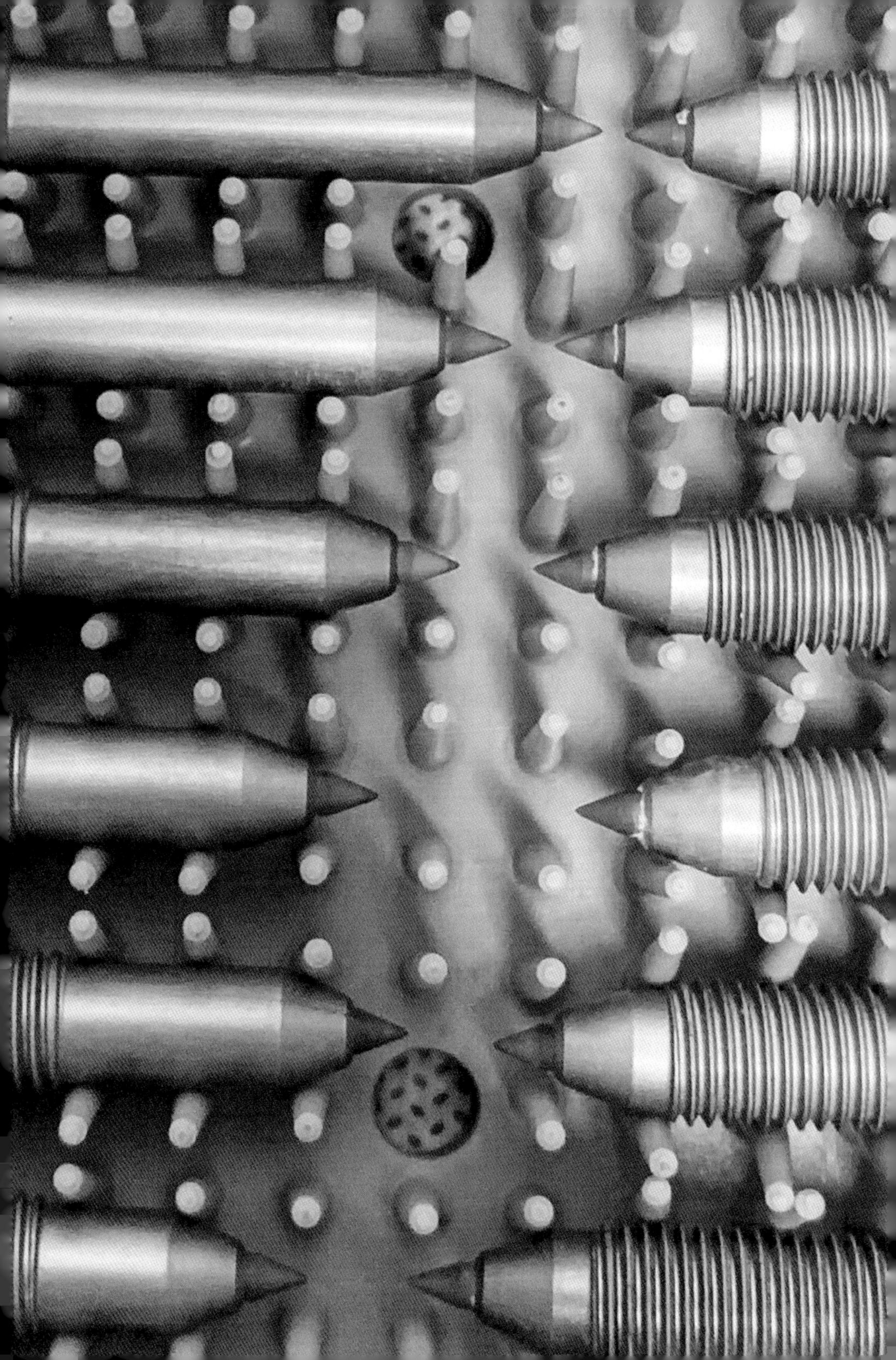

Water Is Life

I used to be fastidious about drinking sixty-four ounces of water each day. Having clear pee left me positively giddy. *Look how responsible I am, a real adult!* I was smug about my water consumption. I had control over my health; going to the bathroom three hundred times a day was a badge of honor, no matter how inconvenient it was. Now it feels like a colossal chore to drink half of that. Cancer affects everything, and when I have so many responsibilities, something as simple as drinking water is one more thing to monitor, one more responsibility. It takes a lot to keep me alive: remembering when to take my chemo pills, keeping up with my multitude of medical appointments. Add a job and grad school on top of that, and I can barely keep up.

Right after I had major surgery to remove my rectum three years ago, I had a temporary ileostomy bag. When you poop out of your stomach via your small intestines, water doesn't get reabsorbed in the colon like it's supposed to. I had to drink water around the clock to make sure I wouldn't get dehydrated.

Shortly after my surgery, Thomas got into a bad Vespa accident. A car was approaching the intersection with no signs of stopping, so he slammed on the brakes and flew off the bike. He shattered his elbow, which required multiple surgeries and a permanent steel plate to keep his elbow together. "I think he left part of his bone on the street," his surgeon said. On the day of the big surgery, my mom and I went to the hospital cafeteria to eat during the operation. A cafeteria employee was mopping the floor and had placed a "wet floor" sign in the walkway. "Don't walk here; the floor is wet," he said. After all that I had been through, I just lost it. "Where am I supposed to walk?" I asked as I burst into tears. "Go sit down," my mom said, pointing to a table.

A year later, I was still dealing with a lot. I described it to my psychiatrist as my bucket is overflowing, and my back-up bucket, and my other back-up bucket. I told her I was running out of buckets. What do you do when the faucet is broken and you can't turn it off?

I started on chemo for a third, unending timeline. I got through more brain radiation and had my melanoma removed. A sliver of my arm was sliced into, excising the cancerous cells. I stopped tracking how much water I drank on my FitBit, but still kept two 32-ounce water bottles full every day.

I wasn't planning to tell anyone at school about my cancer. I had just finished another grad program in May 2020, smack dab in the middle of the pandemic. It was a strange time, not being able to indulge in the pomp and circumstance. I took my own graduation photos with Thomas's help. My favorite one is me in my cap and gown in front of the university sign with a freshly cracked beer. I did the damn thing, graduating on time despite COVID and cancer. I deserved that cold one, despite alcohol being a known carcinogen.

It seems like everything causes cancer. I read somewhere that we eat and drink a credit card's worth of plastic every year. Our drinking water is loaded with all sorts of questionable trace amounts of prescription pills. The pipes under my house are terra-cotta, most likely as old as our one-hundred-year-old home. There are parts of Louisiana called "cancer alley" because of the amount of waste and toxic chemicals in the soil and drinking water.

I tested negative for genetic diseases, but four members of my paternal immediate family have all died from various cancers. Cancer is environmental. Many people claim that diet can prevent cancer, and while that is partially true, it's not the whole story. Health gurus touting claims of downing alkaline water and celery juice as cancer cures are bogus, but people drink it up. Look, I get it. People try to have some semblance of control over their lives. But we have less control over our bodies—hell, over our lives—than we think we do.

After my craniotomy in 2018, I started drinking one hundred ounces of water a day. I thought that if I drank that much water, I would flush the scars out. I would flush all the medication out of my system. I can't recall what specific thing led me to drink that much water, but I eventually tapered off and went back to my normal sixty-four ounces a day. Over the course of four years of treatment, I started to find it difficult to drink plain water. I had to flavor it to trick myself into drinking enough. My mouth was so dry, I'd start chugging it. My body was reanimated as my cells were quenched. I gave up on thinking I have control over my cancer. As a stage-IV patient, there is nothing I can do to make the cancer go away. I'll have this the rest of my life, which makes me feel like giving up on life sometimes. Still, I soldier on, clinging to being alive like a life raft. On my good days I feel almost normal, free of pain and present in the moment. On my bad days, I can barely lift a finger. Still, life is worth living, so I take my chemo pills, kicking them back with a big swig of water. I just hope for the best.

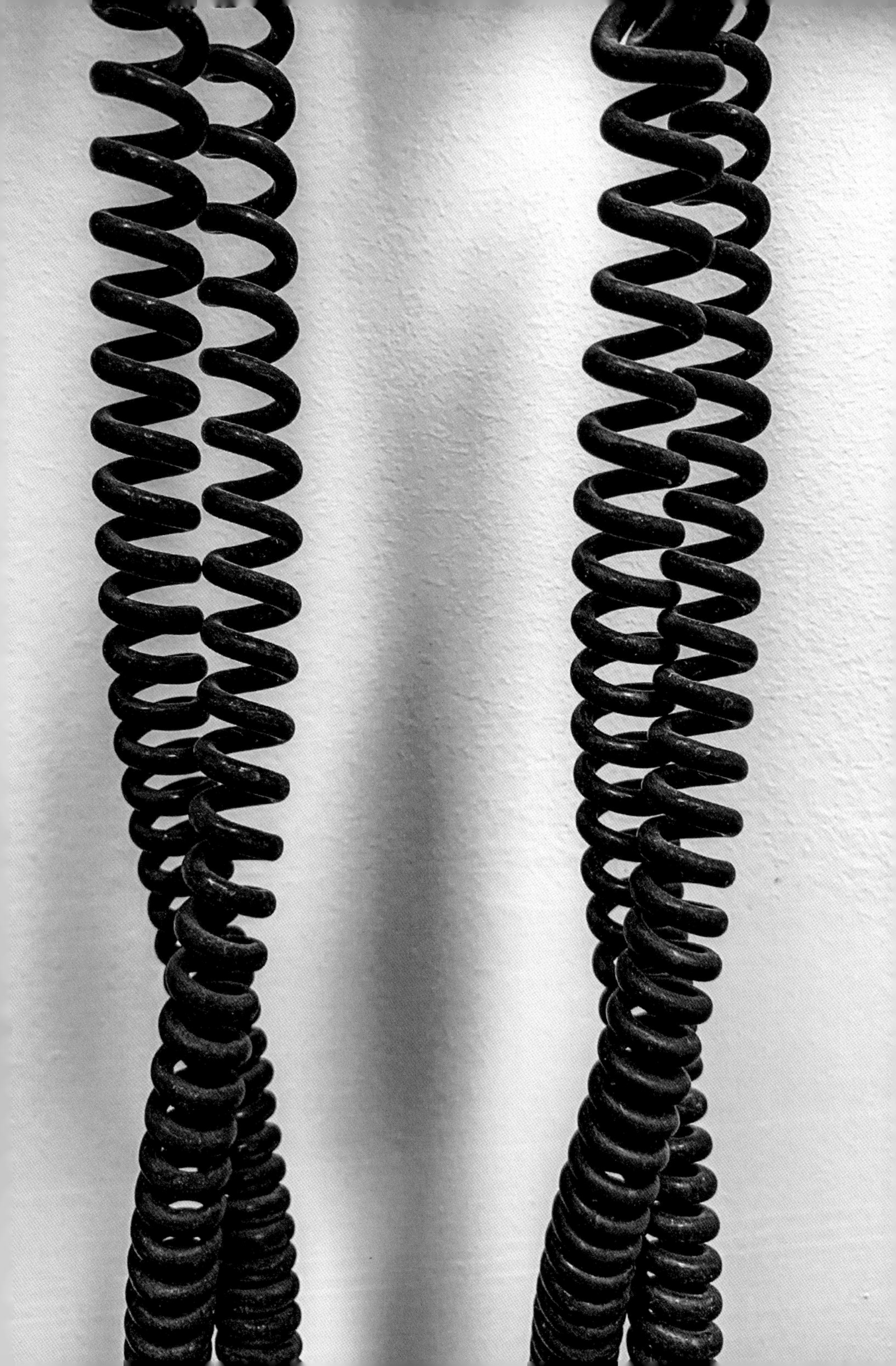

Work

I was interviewing for jobs when I found out my cancer was back. I interviewed at an event space for a server position. It's not that I had a burning desire to wait tables, but it's something that I've done since I was twenty years old. I'm good at the job, for better or worse. When I got the news that I had to go back into treatment, I declined the position because I knew there was no way I'd be able to hold down a regular job. I had worked as a graduate assistant when I was first diagnosed, but that was different. I was already a year into the job by then, so I had already established a relationship there. Starting fresh somewhere that I would have to explain everything wasn't worth it.

I applied for disability instead, which now provides me with a steady check every month. The downside is that I'm capped at how much money I can earn. While I appreciate the disability check, it doesn't feel good being unable to work a steady job. I do the best that I can, picking up freelance writing and photography work as much as possible. I started doing more headshot work, and was booking clients on a regular basis until mid-May, when my eyesight went bad and I had to cancel all of my sessions. Then the summer heat hit and zapped up all of my business. No one wants to have their photo taken outdoors when it's over ninety degrees outside.

While it sounds nice to be a lady of leisure, I need structure in my life. I don't do much when I have too much free time. I float in space, with a vastness that doesn't give me boundaries. I need a slight sense of urgency to get things done. Otherwise, I spend my days doing mindless activities. You don't realize the value of working until you can't. Aside from the money, it feels good to work. I've been able to cobble together a small photography business. And while the sporadic paycheck is nice, it feels better when clients are satisfied with their photos. It feels good to get paid for what you're good at. It's validating.

I also like to be able to financially contribute to my household. Thomas has so much on his plate. He supports us financially and shoulders the burden of my medical bills, in addition to being the main caregiver. It's a lot on him. I try to do as much as I can to contribute. I try to make dinner most nights. Sometimes I'll walk the dog by myself. But sometimes I don't have the energy to do the most basic tasks, like walking into the kitchen for a glass of water. Lately I've been asking him to help me more and more.

I hate feeling dependent on people. Everyday tasks are more difficult because I can't see well. I'm not comfortable riding a bike, plus it's 101 degrees with the heat index, which wouldn't make for a good ride. It's frustrating to feel like I can't take total care of myself. Without Thomas's income, I would be screwed. Disability doesn't pay a living wage, and yet I'm also limited to how much money I can make. Coupled with endless medical debt, I couldn't afford treatment if I was on my own. The entire health-care system is so broken, and I don't have a solution.

We're decidedly middle class, which means we aren't so financially well off that we have nothing to worry about. It also means that we make too much to qualify for low-income services. Cancer is expensive. I realize I'm lucky to have a solid support system, and we make enough to cover my care. But it's nerve-wracking getting an $85,000 bill in the mail. Sure, insurance covers the bulk of it, but it's frightening to see such high amounts owed.

It's incomprehensible to me how people without support, or people living below the poverty line, can endure cancer treatment. I think about people who have to make the harrowing decision to put food on the table or get the treatment they need. After my seizure, I couldn't drive for six months, but I had to maintain my status at the university to keep my health care. I was fortunate to receive two grants that paid for the bulk of my Uber rides back and forth to campus. It cost roughly $2500 for one semester's transportation.

I have to run an errand today, but with the heat index it's 105 degrees outside and I refuse to spend twenty dollars round trip on a five-minute Lyft ride. I acknowledge that this comes from a place of privilege. I could afford the twenty dollars, but I'd rather not spend the money. I used to think about riding my bike to the cancer center. I used to drive myself, or get a ride from someone. But what about people with no options, no way to get to their appointments except for public transportation? I imagine how miserable it must be on a bus, nauseous after treatment. The worst part is being around healthy people who don't get the struggles of being a cancer patient. Hell, even cooking dinner some nights feels like a grand accomplishment. I took so much for granted before I had cancer. The longer I live, the more I realize how much work it takes to keep going. I very much want to stay alive, but it's so hard when your baseline for stress is already through the roof.

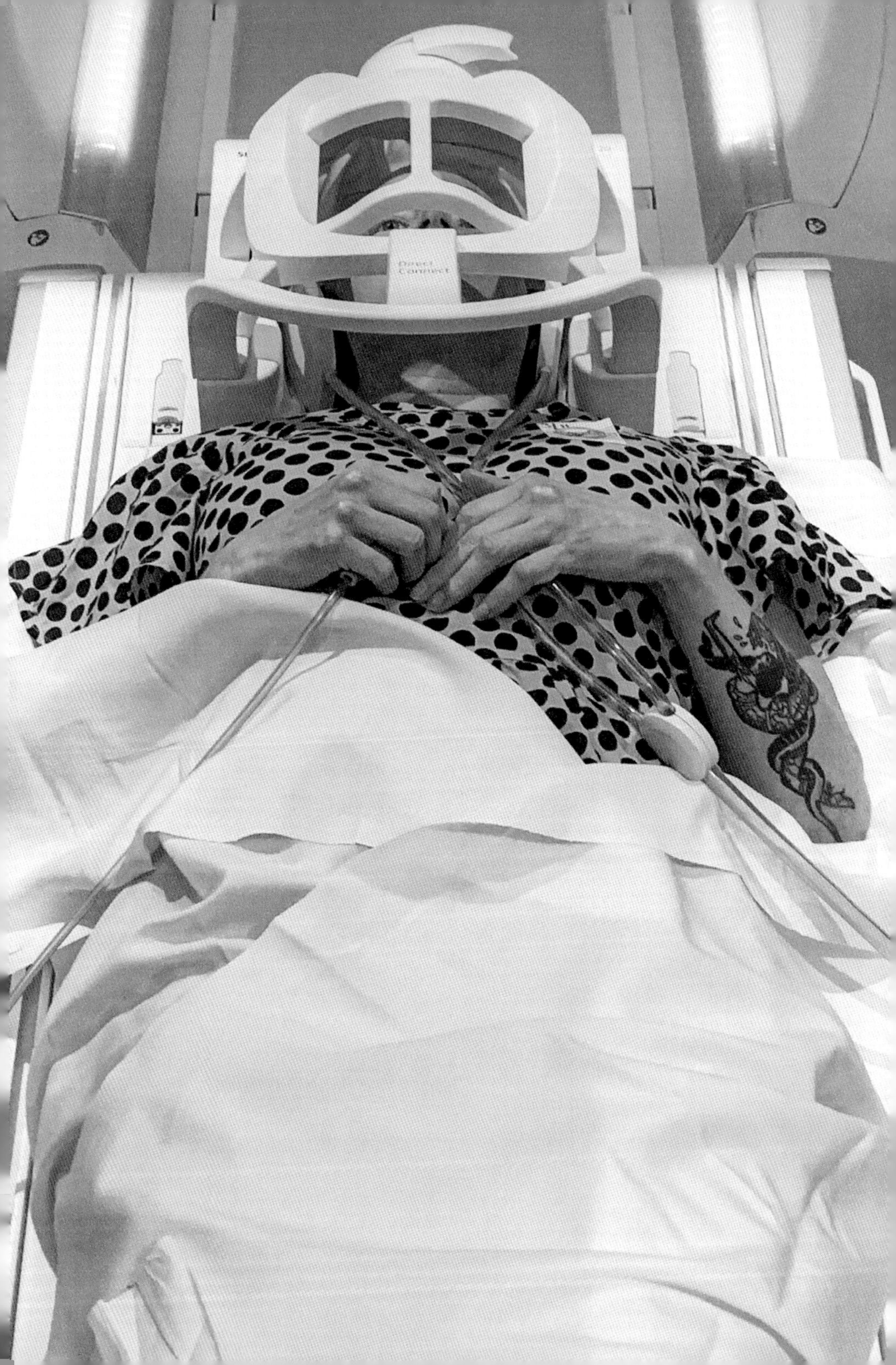

The Deep

I SINK INTO THE WATER, letting the pool take me in. I hadn't been swimming in two weeks because of an unexpected skin biopsy, a measure taken for an atypical mole. My dermatologist wanted to make sure my melanoma hadn't come back. It hadn't, the stitches came out, and now I'm able to swim again. However, my eyesight is having problems again. I can see, but everything is off, like trying to see through an electrical spark.

Still, the cool water feels good on my body. I extend my arms, holding on to my kick board and push off the pool wall, enjoying the weightlessness as my legs propel me to the deep end. I feel free in the water despite the burden of perpetual cancer treatment slowly breaking down my body. Everything was already heavy before my eyes went bad, but I was coasting along with stable tumors. I am used to this. I am used to living my life in three-month increments, from scan to medical scan. My life literally depends on these, to monitor the cancer. My best-case scenario is that it remains stable, that everything stays in place. I am in a relatively good place, two months out from learning that it's my time to go.

I am suspended in the deep end, my face hovering above the water before I kick my legs again, trying to get my body parallel with the board. I focus on my form, trying to optimize my forty-five-minute workout. The only goal I have is to swim twice a week. I don't care about improving my speed. I'm not competing with anyone, not even myself. I'm learning how to do things for the pure joy of it, something that makes me feel good.

My eyes get used to swimming without my glasses. I can read the time: 10:05 a.m. I've got about forty minutes to go. I kick back to the shallow end and ditch the kick board, lunging into a backstroke. I tilt my pelvis to the ceiling, trying to remain upright. I bend my arms, tapping into the ballet classes I took as a child.

I use my hands to scoop the water, trying to be graceful and strong. My feet flutter through the water. Chemo has gnarled my hands and feet and left them in an endless cycle of inflammation. Even standing in the pool hurts sometimes.

My fingers tap the wall. I just finished another lap. I use the base of the spring board to do ten pull-ups, something I couldn't do out of the water. I was so strong before my cancer diagnosis four years ago—hitting the gym three times a week, running 5K races. That strength is still there, hidden in muscle tendons, but activating it grows harder and harder the more chemo I have, the longer I stay alive.

Chemo is a double-edged sword. It's kept me alive four years, but it's also breaking me down. I try my best to stay active, but my obstacles seem insurmountable at times. I've made peace with never looking or feeling as good as I did before I started treatment, but it's hard knowing I'll never get back to the shape I was in, feeling good about myself.

It's not that I feel bad about myself, but life is so difficult. I switch from backstrokes to side strokes, enjoying the way my torso stretches, unfolding in ways that lengthen my body. I can never figure out if I'm supposed to kick with the leg that is on top of the water, or the one that acts as an anchor below the surface. I alternate, letting my arms rest. When I flip back around, my left arm, the one that holds a scar from melanoma surgery, is underneath me. Melanoma, a secondary cancer I had, prevents me from qualifying in clinical trials. I have to be melanoma-free for five years. It's been a year and a half, but that doesn't matter much to me. By the time I qualify, I will be dead.

I stop between laps to do twenty kickbacks. I press my feet against the wall of the pool, then thrust my legs back, working my abdominal muscles. My stoma scar is hidden underneath my bathing suit, but I know it's there. All that's left of my small intestines hanging out of my stomach for nine weeks is a memory and a scar. Getting sliced open three years ago was brutal. You don't know how much you rely on your abs for basic functions, such as standing up, until you have abdominal surgery. I swim to strengthen my core, to nourish my body. I'm reminded daily of how hard it is to remain alive. Simply walking up a flight of stairs winds me, but cardio in the water feels good. I expand my lungs, opening my body up to the possibility that I might outlive many of my cancer-patient friends.

I grab my kick board, trying to get in a few more laps before my forty-five minutes comes to an end. Swimming is pure joy for me. I can take my mind off cancer, focusing on what my body is capable of instead of what it can't do anymore. The water is cool and pleasant as I glide through the water, as my legs propel me in the lane.

During my last minute, I stretch my limbs. I work out any stiffness, starting with pulling calf muscles, then my thighs and my arms. I always forget to stretch my neck. There is always some body part that I neglect, which is why I like swimming so much. It's a full body workout, strengthening my core, my limbs, and my mind. It's one of my few escapes from reality.

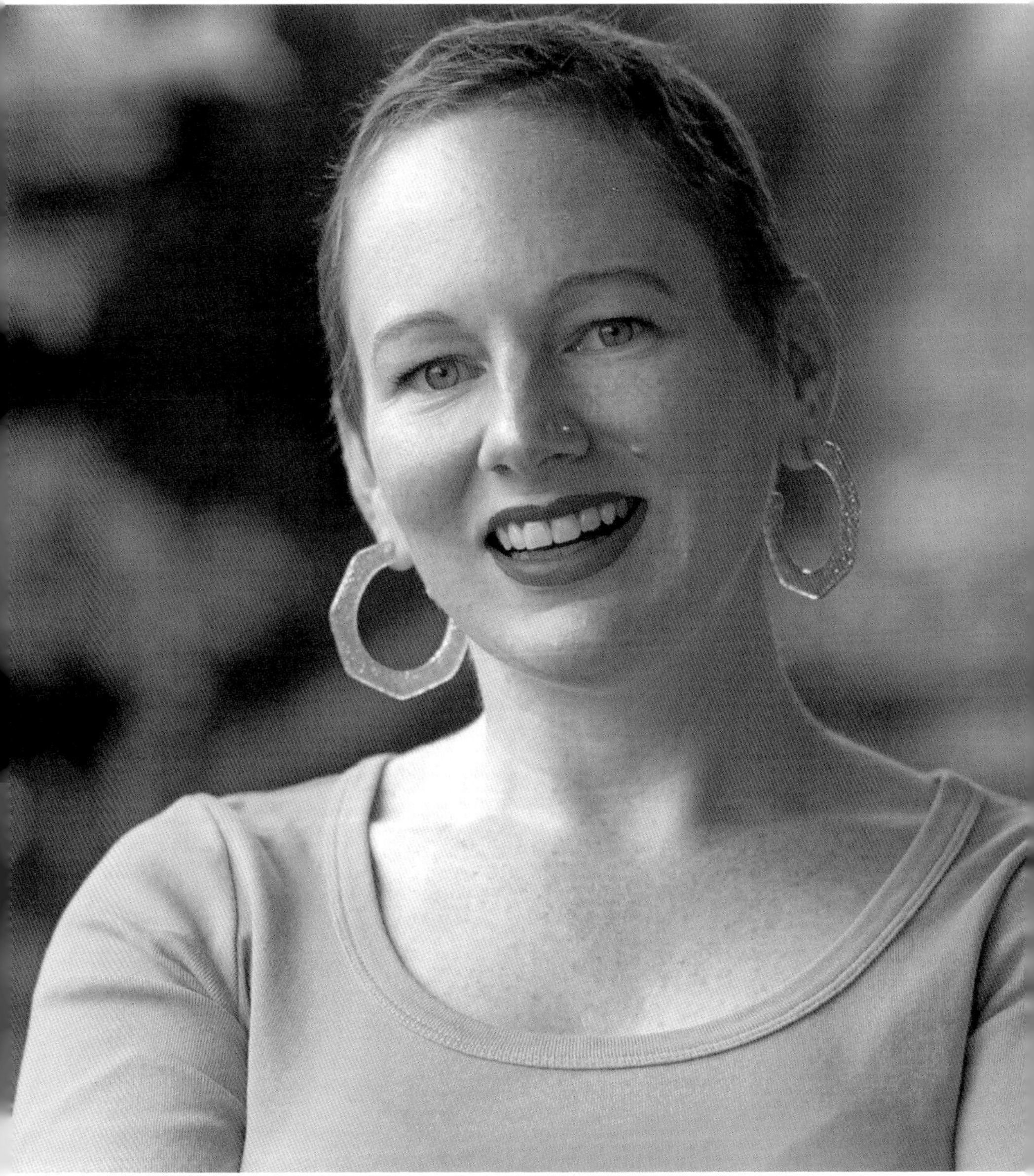

Christy Lorio (1980–2022) was a writer and photographer based in New Orleans, Louisiana. In 2021, Christy was a fellow at Arizona State University's Desert Nights, Rising Stars Writing Conference. Her writing has appeared in *Had*, *433 Magazine*, and *Oxford American*, among other places. Her photography has been seen in publications such as *Vice News* and *In These Times*. Her fine art has been shown in galleries both internationally and nationally, including the Ogden Museum of Southern Art and Good Children Gallery in New Orleans. Christy earned an MFA in creative writing from the University of New Orleans.